THE
ETHICAL
PLANNING
PRACTITIONER

THE ETHICAL PLANNING PRACTITIONER

Jerry Weitz, FAICP, PhD

Routledge
Taylor & Francis Group

LONDON AND NEW YORK

First published 2015 by the American Planning Association

Published 2017 by Routledge
4 Park Square, Milton Park, Abingdon, Oxon OX14 4RN
605 Third Avenue, New York, NY 10017

Routledge is an imprint of the Taylor & Francis Group, an informa business

ISBN: 978-1-138-73521-7 (pbk)

Library of Congress Control Number: 2015944995

*In memory of my father, John Jerome Weitz (1926–2011),
and mother, Marcheta Knight Weitz (1934–2002)*

CONTENTS

INTRODUCTION

The AICP Code and APA Ethical Principles in Planning

The American Institute of Certified Planners (AICP) is the professional institute of the American Planning Association (APA). Planners with the AICP credential support adherence to the AICP Code of Ethics and Professional Conduct (AICP Code), which is provided in full in Appendix A of this book. The AICP Code was completely rewritten and readopted in 2005, and amended again in 2009. Planners who are not members of AICP are not subject to the AICP Code and its enforcement provisions for violations of rules of conduct. Yet non-certified planners are expected to follow APA's Ethical Principles in Planning (adopted by the APA Board in 1992), even if there is no enforcement arm to ensure adherence.

APA's Ethical Principles in Planning are very similar to the AICP Code in most respects. The individual actions of planners, whether certified or not, reflect on the profession as a whole. This means that all professional planners, not just those who are AICP-certified, have professional obligations to conduct themselves ethically and with integrity. While the AICP code and the APA ethical principles are in most cases congruent, there are unique obligations on AICP members to take action, urge policy and regulatory change, and make sure that participation is not just a superficial opportunity but an activity that seriously influences policy and affects people beneficially. There is also a "promptness" principle applicable to AICP members that is not explicit in the APA Ethical Principles in Planning. AICP planners are also uniquely charged with pursuing certain ends—namely, social justice, racial integration, and excellence of design. AICP planners must "urge the alteration of policies, institutions, and decisions that oppose needs of the disadvantaged," and they must ensure, in participation processes, that all affected groups have an opportunity not just for participation per se but "for meaningful impact" (AICP Code). AICP planners must also work to expand choice and opportunity for all persons, an aspiration not contained in the APA Ethical Principles in Planning.

The AICP Code is organized in four sections: A, B, C, and D. Sections A and B only are emphasized here: Section A, Principles to Which We Aspire, and Section B, Our Rules of Conduct. Section C, Our Code Procedures, describes how to obtain informal and formal advice on ethics questions but is devoted mostly to the procedures of raising and adjudicating misconduct charges. Section D, Planners Convicted of Serious Crimes—Automatic Suspension of Certification, was added by amendment to the AICP Code in 2009; that section defines "serious crime" and describes the obligations of and consequences to the certified planner when convicted of a serious crime. This book is based on the current AICP Code of Ethics and Professional Conduct. However, the AICP Ethics Committee periodically reviews the code and recommends revisions to the AICP Commission and APA membership. Proposed changes in the next version of the code will affect and draw from what are now Sections C and D. These sections will be revised and reorganized into three new sections: Section C, Advisory Opinions; Section D, Adjudication of Complaints and Misconduct; and Section E: Discipline of Members. The final approval of these changes would occur in 2016.

As indicated in the preamble of the AICP Code, planners with the AICP credential must "strive to act in accordance" with the principles articulated in Section A, but failure to achieve the principles "cannot be the subject of a misconduct charge or be a cause for disciplinary action." Certified planners are held accountable to the rules of conduct in Section B. Violation of a rule described in Section B of the AICP Code can lead to a charge of misconduct and, if blameworthy, a certified planner can be subject to sanctions, including loss of the AICP credential. Clearly, this places emphasis on planners abiding by the rules of conduct (Section B), since the rules are enforceable, but the AICP Code clearly intends that certified planners aspire to meet the principles articulated in Section A of the AICP Code.

AICP introduced its certification maintenance requirements in 2008. They require AICP members to complete 32 hours of continuing education every two years, including 1.5 hours on the subject of ethics. The last book APA published that emphasizes the ethical aspirations and obligations of the AICP Code was Carol Barrett's *Everyday Ethics for Practicing Planners* (APA Planners Press 2002), and that book preceded the overhaul of the AICP Code in 2005. APA (2012) has prepared a revised toolkit on conducting ethics training sessions and has also distributed an "ethics case of the year" in recent years, to help fill the need for certification maintenance in ethics. Despite the utility of these works, there continues to be an increasing need for material to use in educating professional planners about ethics. The 76 ethics scenarios provided in this book can be introduced and discussed in ethics training sessions, as well as in undergraduate and graduate planning courses with content on ethics. This book can also be used by individual practicing planners to heighten their awareness of various ethical issues and possible ways to respond to them. Planners who need a reference source on ethics in preparing for the AICP certification examination will also find this book useful in gaining familiarity with applications of the AICP Code in practical contexts.

Principles to Which We Aspire
Table 1 provides generalized summaries of the principles to which we aspire (Section A of the AICP Code).

Table 1. AICP Code Principles to Which We Aspire, Quick Reference Guide

1. Responsibility to the Public

1.a. Consider rights of others
1.b. Concern for long-range consequences
1.c. Attend to interrelatedness of decisions
1.d. Provide information to all affected
1.e. Participation—meaningful impact
1.f. Social justice—plan for disadvantaged
1.g. Excellent design; preserve heritage
1.h. Deal fairly and evenhandedly

2. Responsibility to Clients/Employers

2.a. Exercise independent judgment
2.b. Accept client decision unless illegal . . .
2.c. Avoid appearance of conflict of interest

3. Responsibility to Profession/Colleagues

3.a. Enhance professional integrity
3.b. Educate public on planning issues
3.c. Treat other professionals fairly
3.d. Share experience and research
3.e. Apply customary solutions with caution
3.f. Contribute to professional development
3.g. Increase opportunity for underrepresented groups
3.h. Enhance education and training
3.i. Examine/analyze ethical issues
3.j. Contribute to those lacking resources

As indicated in Table 1, the 21 principles to which we aspire (Section A of the AICP Code) are organized into three areas of responsibility: to the public, to clients and employers, and to the profession and colleagues.

Rules of Conduct
The rules of conduct of the AICP Code are numbered 1 through 26 and referred to in this book as B.1 through B.26. The rules of conduct do not come with descriptive titles. Generalizing the rules helps one to remember them more easily and to refer to them with some brevity. Table 2 provides a generalization of the 26 rules of conduct for purposes of easy reference. However, you should consult the actual rules (The AICP

Code is provided in its entirety in Appendix A) rather than rely on the generalizations provided in Table 2, which cannot substitute for frequent consultation of the full language of the rules in Section B of the AICP Code.

Table 2. AICP Code Rules of Conduct, Quick Reference Guide

1. Inaccurate information—untruthfulness
2. Illegal or unethical conduct
3. Change of public position on an issue
4. Outside employment ("moonlighting")
5. Acceptance of gifts or advantage
6. Personal or financial gain
7. Breach of confidentiality
8. Private communication (public)
9. Private communication (other)
10. Misrepresentation of others' qualifications
11. Solicitation via false claims; duress
12. Misstatement of one's qualifications
13. Influence via improper means
14. Official power used for advantage
15. Work beyond professional competence
16. Promptness of work required
17. Misuse of others' work
18. Pressure: unsubstantiated findings
19. Concealment of interest/failure to disclose
20. Unlawful discrimination
21. Cooperation in AICP investigation
22. Retaliation for misconduct charge
23. Threat to file charge (advantage)
24. No frivolous ethics charge
25. Deliberate, wrongful act
26. Notification of "serious crime"

The Ethical Conduct of Planners

There is no concrete evidence I am aware of that suggests planners are an unethical bunch. To the contrary, one of the few indicators of the level of unethical behavior is the number of planners sanctioned for misconduct by AICP's ethics officer per the AICP Code. In that regard, the numbers of sanctions seem very small, and there appear to be relatively few examples in our profession's history of pervasive ethical misconduct by planners. Of course, that single measure (i.e., the number of planners sanctioned over time) does not necessarily indicate ethical behavior or the absence of misconduct, since unethical behavior could go unnoticed or unsanctioned. The very existence of the AICP Code may be evidence of the need for one. And one might even consider AICP's mandate that its members continue their education, including ethics, as some evidence of prior professional misconduct. On the other hand, the AICP Code and AICP's certification maintenance requirements might be considered simply to be proactive or preventative measures, rather than reactions to a discrete and identifiable trend of ethical misconduct among planners.

While there may be a lack of evidence of pervasive misconduct among planners, we do know that a sizable share of professional planners are employed by governments, especially local governments.

Ethical problems in government include fraud, waste, abuse of government funds, abuse of the public trust, improper acceptance of gifts for political favors, and failure to disclose conflicts of interest, among others. Some government employees use their positions and the services they deliver to the public as vehicles for personal gain and increased power, manipulating the system for maximum benefit to themselves, family, friends, or business associates (Steinberg and Austern 1990). Unethical behavior can shake public confidence in government, to the detriment of all planners as they do their jobs.

Furthermore, there is evidence that unethical behavior is more prevalent among employees at the local level than among state and federal government employees. One in four government employees work in an environment conducive to misconduct, and one in seven have indicated they have had to compromise ethics standards in the course of their jobs (Ethics Resource Center 2008). Indeed, local government planners are susceptible to the pressures that can lead to compromised ethics, and they are front and center when it comes to some serious legal and ethical dangers. For example, because government land-use decisions can result in windfalls and wipeouts for property owners, zoning bribes are among the largest offered to public officials (Steinberg and Austern 1990). Hence, without unduly indicting the planning profession, it is clear that the potential for ethical misconduct by planners is omnipresent, at least among those of us employed by local governments.

Guidance for Ethical Decision Making

Acting ethically requires serious, considerable effort, more time than many planners probably anticipate. Planners should not assume that ethical decision making is limited to quick determinations of legality and compliance with rules of conduct of the AICP Code, with passing consideration of the "principles to which we aspire." Where rules are evident, the advice seems simple: Follow them. But everything ethical or unethical cannot be articulated in rules.

As I note in commentaries to the scenarios, some of the rules of conduct are written with a limited context and can thus be literally interpreted as inapplicable to a given situation when certain factual contexts do not exist. The strict construction of a given rule of conduct may lead a planner to conclude that the rule has not been violated. In my view, strict construction of rules of conduct may lead to the planner rationalizing that such contemplated behavior is not unethical, given the narrow language of a given rule. I urge planners to consider the intent of the rules of conduct and to apply them in broader contexts. In the commentaries to the scenarios, I identify several instances where I believe the spirit—but not the very limited context—of the code can be violated. In a later section, I provide "interpretations" of certain words and phrases and again urge planners to go beyond minimum expectations of compliance with rules of conduct of the AICP Code, as strictly construed. I also provide conclusions about the characteristics of the ethical planning practitioner. As noted in the conclusion, the ethical planning practitioner will consider rules of conduct and principles potentially applicable, even if the strict construction of them might lead others to dismiss them as irrelevant. In offering interpretations, I hope to elevate the standard of ethics beyond a minimalist or legalistic approach.

Scenarios: Introduction and Guidance

This book includes 76 scenarios, numbered consecutively for reference purposes. The scenarios are written to help planners understand how the principles and rules of the AICP Code might apply to situations in which they find themselves. Several of the scenarios included in this book were presented during ethics sessions I organized at APA's National Planning Conferences in Los Angeles (2012) and in Chicago (2013). Others are drawn from the APA *Ethics Session Toolkit* (2012) and the planning ethics literature. Many of the scenarios are based on my own experience, while others are hypothetical.

Each scenario follows a similar format. First, a situation (scenario) is presented. Second, principles and rules from the AICP Code that appear to be relevant are identified; note that generalized references to relevant or potentially relevant principles and rules are presented in table form to avoid reiterating them over and over again verbatim each time they are relevant. If a principle or rule appears in the table for the scenario, it means that (1) I considered such a principle or rule to be relevant (sometimes under additional assumptions or contingencies not given in the scenario) and (2) its applicability or potential applicability is described in the commentary. You are encouraged to go through the scenarios and think systematically about whether any other principles or rules apply. There is always the possibility that you will find another principle or rule relevant to the scenario, even though I have not cited it.

Third, I provide commentary as to which principles and rules may apply and for what reasons. The commentary also provides some opinions as to what might be considered ethical and unethical behavior (e.g., whether or not a certain action violates one or more principles or one or more rules of conduct). Frequently, I suggest what I would do in the given situation. The commentaries are by no means definitive—they represent only my own opinion, which cannot be considered authoritative. In many instances, the commentary poses more questions about the applicability of AICP code principles and rules of conduct. Several scenarios also include a "for further discussion" section, which has additional questions you may choose to contemplate.

The scenarios are generally grouped by content and related situations, starting with those that evoke the code's principles and then those that relate primarily to rules of conduct. However, many of the scenarios involve a mix of principles and rules. Further, in many instances, multiple principles and multiple rules are relevant in a given scenario. For these reasons, the scenarios defy organization. The ethical planning practitioner will sort out these complexities, with the understanding that the rules of conduct govern. An index of scenarios by principle and rule of conduct is provided at the end of this book and can be consulted as appropriate.

Number of Scenarios per Training Session

Ethics training sessions are usually scheduled for 1.5 hours to meet AICP's certification maintenance requirements. The number of scenarios that can be considered in a given training session will depend on the number of respondents, the degree of audience interaction, the complexity of the scenarios, and the amount of information covered in the introduction and conclusion. Eight to 10 scenarios can typically be included in one 90-minute session, given modest audience interaction.

Selecting Scenarios

For general ethics training sessions, or for planning courses, it is recommended that a diverse range of scenarios be selected so that broad coverage of the AICP Code is achieved. When choosing which scenarios to include in a training session, consult the index of scenarios by principle and by rule to facilitate diverse coverage.

The scenarios can be used in many ways. Individual planners, planning professors, and ethics session organizers will have their own philosophy and preferences for how to use the scenarios and how to organize content of ethics instruction sessions and lessons. I offer several observations and recommendations for using the scenarios.

For Individual Planners

For individual planners, the ideal learning experience, in my view, is to read a given scenario, then ask yourself *which principles and rules of conduct apply to this scenario*. Because you probably have not memorized all 21 principles and 26 rules of conduct, you should read through Sections A and B of the AICP Code to *identify for yourself* which principles and rules of conduct might apply to the situation. I recommend that you not go straight to the list of principles and rules that are identified as relevant. Also, don't read the commentary provided yet.

Why should you follow this advice? Because the preamble of the AICP Code indicates that "an ethical judgment often requires a conscientious balancing, based on the facts and context of a particular situation and on the *precepts of the entire Code*" [emphasis added]. Also, Section A, Principle 3 (i) of the AICP Code states that "We [planners with the AICP credential] *shall systematically and critically analyze* ethical issues in the practice of planning" [emphasis added]; you may not recognize an ethics issue exists unless you examine all of the principles and rules of conduct carefully.

After reviewing the principles and rules in the AICP Code and considering their applicability to the given scenario, you can then proceed to other steps, such as comparing your own list of principles and rules you found relevant with the table of principles and rules listed as relevant. After considering the relevance of principles and rules of conduct, you can then decide whether or not it would be ethical to engage in the particular activity posed in the scenario, or you may consult the commentary and consider my view and any additional questions raised therein. Remember, my commentary is just an opinion, one that is by no means authoritative.

For Ethics Session Organizers
After presenting a scenario, the question that should be asked first, for every scenario, is *which principles and rules of conduct apply to this scenario.* This is a standing question for each scenario, and although it is not repeated for each scenario here, it should be asked after each scenario presented in training sessions. Participants should be directed (and if possible, given the time required) to examine the contents of Sections A and B of the AICP Code and identify for themselves which principles and rules apply to the given scenario. There is no substitute for or shortcut to systematically examining the code with the facts of the scenario in mind.

However, due to time constraints, organized sessions on ethics (usually 90 minutes long) will be different from how individuals will use the scenarios. It is customary (at least in my experience) for an ethics session organizer to read through a scenario, then identify those principles and rules of conduct that appear to have relevance to the given situation. This may be necessary given the time allowed. Again, however, if the planning course instructor or session moderator identifies relevant principles and rules on behalf of participants, they will miss the real experience of identifying and critically analyzing ethical issues on their own, starting with their own identification of relevant principles and rules of conduct.

If it is not realistic to afford time during the session for individuals to read Sections A and B of the Code (so that they can identify, on their own, principles and rules of conduct relevant to the scenario), there is a second-best alternative: display Tables 1 and 2 (see the Introduction), which provide quick reference guides to the principles and rules, respectively, and ask for participants to identify relevant or potentially relevant principles and rules of conduct.

The second-best alternative—giving time for participants to identify from the summary tables those principles and rules that apply to a given scenario—may also be too time consuming, particularly if there are panelists or discussants who are offering their views. In such instances where time cannot be given to audience participation, or where panel speakers will weigh in, it is appropriate (as a third alternative) to simply display the principles and rules of conduct I have identified as relevant or potentially relevant.

Once the relevant principles and rules have been identified for the scenario, the instructor or session facilitator can proceed to a discussion of ethics decision making, including options and alternatives for actions that planners can use when addressing the ethics issue. If the session is designed for maximum participation, observers can be called upon to comment about how they would respond. If panelists are included, they can then give their opinions and ideas for whether the action contemplated in the scenario is consistent or inconsistent with the AICP Code, and why.

I believe it is especially important not to include a set of predetermined alternative courses of action (e.g., choose "a" through "d"), and the commentaries do not provide such predetermined actions. Why? Again, in my view, participants need to think about and determine their own responses to a given ethics issue rather than being given a fixed set of possible responses. We should not take away the individual's ingenuity and opportunity for critical thinking; we would be doing so if predetermined answers are provided. In the commentaries following each scenario, I provide my own view of how to respond to each situation. Frequently, however, there will be a range of possible responses. The commentaries I provide often include a recommended action, which should only be viewed by the planner or disclosed to session participants after they have had their own opportunity to determine the best course of action. Frequently, the commentaries will raise further questions or ask the planner to consider whether a given principle or rule might apply given additional assumptions or under certain specific additional circumstances. Remember that any actions recommended in the commentary are not definitive or authoritative, and they must not be construed as advice to participants.

In my experience, planners attending ethics training sessions are often eager to share their own ethical dilemmas. One way I've accommodated this is to bring index cards and ask attendees at the beginning of the session to write down their own ethics questions for consideration by the session organizer or panelists. The questions can then be collected and read aloud, and panelists or the audience (or both, time permitting) can respond.

I stop short of recommending and including specific scenarios for training, but the session organizer can use the index of scenarios in this book to select scenarios in a way that ensures diverse coverage of different principles and rules of conduct. For helpful guidance on options for organizing ethics training sessions, see APA (2012).

SCENARIOS

1

Disagreement With Supervisor's Recommendation

A planning director for a local government has developed draft land-use policies in a proposed comprehensive plan that have the support of a few vocal, politically and financially connected community members. The vast majority of the public does not support these policies. You are a junior-level planner and believe that the planning director's draft land-use policies promote exclusionary zoning and create an unnecessary cost burden to provide inefficient infrastructure. You approach the planning director and express your views, suggesting that changes to the policies are needed. The planning director, however, is not persuaded and refuses to change the draft land-use policies. What should you do now? (Carolin, Gerhart-Fritz, and Weitz 2012)

Commentary

Your options appear to be (1) accept the planning director's decision not to revisit the land-use policies, or (2) dissent. Your action strategy depends on just how strong your convictions are. Even though the planning director disagrees with you, you still have a right, perhaps even some responsibility, to educate the public about planning issues (3.b), including how the land-use plan is relevant to everyday lives (2.b). In this scenario you have to decide which principle is most important: responsibility to the employer and client, or responsibility to the public. The planning director is your supervisor, but the ethical planning practitioner does not lose sight of multiple clients, including the public generally. Ethical planning practitioners can exercise dissent if their convictions are so strong that they feel compelled to do so, and if they have done the analysis to justify those convictions. Dissent strategies could include discussing the policy disagreement with the planning director's supervisor or attempting to rally people in opposition to the policies. If you decide to dissent, consider the tactics carefully, since each dissent tactic can have its own consequences and ethical overtones. If you elect to dissent, you need to be fair and professional in arguing against the planning director's position (3.c). I would probably not exercise dissent in this instance, since I've already exercised independent judgment (2.a), and because there is some prospect that the public will rise in opposition to the draft land-use policies without prodding or encouragement on my part. I would not attempt to rally the public against the draft land-use policies, given my junior position, and since an appearance of subterfuge or insubordination could damage my relationship with my boss and potentially reduce my influence in the future.

Relevant AICP Code Provisions

Principles to Which We Aspire

2.a. Exercise independent judgment
2.b. Accept client decision unless illegal . . .
3.b. Educate public on planning issues
3.c. Treat other professionals fairly

2

Conflict with Supervisor

You are the planning manager for a local government. Your immediate supervisor is not an AICP member and holds the politically appointed role of community and economic development director, a position that advocates for growth. The director often sees things from the applicant's point of view. As the planning manager, you find that the director looks for ways to bypass zoning and development code provisions, reinterpret code, or otherwise soft-pedal the land-use regulations. One or more members of the public and local government staff bring this up as an issue. Is there any course of action for you to take other than implementing the zoning and development code honestly? (Carolin, Gerhart-Fritz, and Weitz 2012)

Commentary

Zoning and development code administration may not be considered a "planning process," but in my view the code should be interpreted more broadly to encompass zoning administration and other processes involving planners. You cannot deal evenhandedly with all zoning applicants (1.h) if the director exercises undue administrative discretion with regard to zoning and land-development codes in favor of economic development. A continued lack of evenhandedness on the part of the director will likely cause increasing discontent. Rezoning and development proposals that don't create economic development deserve the same interpretations of zoning codes that are given to applicants of projects that do stimulate the economy. Nor can you exercise independent judgment (2.a), or at least effectuate that judgment, if the director is prone to overruling you. Furthermore, you cannot act diligently and competently under such circumstances. Hence, the situation must be confronted.

One option is for you to discuss the issue with the director, inform her of your dissatisfaction, and ask for an improvement of relations so that you can function appropriately in your job. Another option is for you to report the problem to the director's supervisor. The director is politically appointed in this scenario, so her supervisor would be the local governing body or local government manager. In doing so, you need to be cognizant of principle 3.c and be fair in commenting about the activities of the director. While not solving the immediate ethical problems, your discussions with the governing body or manager about the inherent and explicit conflicts that arise when development administration comes under the same authority as community and economic development could lead to a local government reorganization of those functions so that the integrity of both can be preserved. Yet another option might be to contact the local government's legal counsel and seek direction or even intervention.

Rule of conduct 2 indicates that "We shall not accept an assignment from a client or employer when the services to be

Relevant AICP Code Provisions

Principles to Which We Aspire

1.h. Deal fairly and evenhandedly

2.a. Exercise independent judgment

2.b. Accept client decision unless illegal . . .

3.c. Treat other professionals fairly

Rules of Conduct

2. Illegal or unethical conduct

performed involve conduct that we know to be illegal or in violation of these rules." If you continue with your job under the present circumstances, you are accepting an assignment under circumstances where conduct (the director's, not your own) is apparently unlawful: The director is interpreting local laws (zoning and development codes) in a way that is inconsistent with their strict construction and context—at least in your view as the planning manager. You would be right to insist that your development code administrative assignment not continue under the present circumstances, because continuing your job under the circumstances would involve accepting future assignments involving conduct that you believe is unlawful (because an adopted law is not being followed). Perhaps you even have an obligation under rule of conduct 2 to remedy the situation or quit the job if a satisfactory and ethical solution cannot be prescribed.

Principle 2.b raises an interesting question about loyalty. To some extent, the director's staff should be expected to defer to her overall direction of the department, including administrative discretion. The director has a conception of economic development as a primary public interest, and judging by her job title, the department was set up with economic development in mind. However, it is apparent in this scenario that the director is taking far too much liberty in zoning and development code administration. It is much better to change the laws in favor of economic development if that is the sentiment of the community, rather than bend the code, because that can lead to inconsistent and therefore incompetent administration. In my view, you should attach loyalty to the local governing body, which is ultimately responsible and accountable, not to the position of department director.

Proposed Change to First Redraft of Official Zoning Map

You are a planner working for a small town that has an outdated zoning ordinance and official zoning map. While you are presenting your redraft of the official zoning map to the town's planning commission during a work session, with no public or media in attendance, one of the members of the planning commission articulates a desire to change the zoning designation on property he owns. He takes a pen out and changes his property on the draft zoning map from single-family residential to commercial zoning. None of the other planning commission members in attendance say or do anything; they remain frozen. How do you respond to the planning commissioner's proposal?

Commentary

The town planning commissioner has capitalized on an opportunity to influence a public decision-making process to serve his own interests. Arguably, the commissioner has a duty to provide input and may legitimately make recommendations and suggestions. In this case, however, the commissioner is advocating for his own real property interests, which could clearly be considered a conflict of interest.

Principle 2.c reads: "We shall avoid a conflict of interest or even the appearance of a conflict of interest in accepting assignments from clients or employers." It is not you who is engaged in a conflict (or potential conflict) of interest, but the principle is not necessarily limited to your own conduct. You have significant influence and responsibility in this public process, and the ethical planner will aspire per principle 2.c to avoid an appearance of a conflict of interest, even one that is not your own.

The planning commissioner's action may be unlawful in some states. You should check the law for planning commissioner ethics in your state, if there is one (see Appendix B for a summary of ethics laws at the state level). For example, in Arizona, it appears that the planning commissioner's action would be unlawful. Or you might ask the town's attorney for an opinion in the matter. If it is determined to be unlawful for the planning commissioner to engage in a conflict of interest, would you be violating rule of conduct 2 if you acquiesce to the planning commissioner's demand? In my view, yes; the planner would violate rule of conduct 2 in a state that had a law making the planning commissioner's action unlawful, because unless you object and refuse you would be accepting an assignment from a client which involves conduct you have confirmed is illegal.

I would refuse to do what the commissioner suggests. Refusal to cooperate is especially appropriate if it is confirmed that the action is unlawful, but one could also justify a refusal

Relevant AICP Code Provisions

Principles to Which We Aspire

2.b. Accept client decision unless illegal . . .

2.c. Avoid appearance of conflict of interest

Rules of Conduct

2. Illegal or unethical conduct

to cooperate based on the aspiration to avoid a conflict of interest. If I were a planner in a state where the action is not clearly unlawful, I would inform the planning commissioner that I will not make the requested change because it is inconsistent with principle 2.c.

For Further Discussion

What about principle 2.b? It reads: "We shall accept the decisions of our client or employer concerning the objectives and nature of the professional services we perform unless the course of action is illegal or plainly inconsistent with our primary obligation to the public interest." If the planning commissioner's action is not illegal, the planner has to determine if the professional services requested are plainly inconsistent with the primary obligation to the public interest. This may be so, on the basis of inconsistency with principle 2.c. In the absence of such a finding by the planner, should the planner aspire to accept the planning commissioner's action because he is the client? I think not. The town itself is the client, and the commissioner is just one member of a board that advises the client.

4

Protection of Environmentally Sensitive Land from Development

You are a consulting land planner, and your client has asked you to prepare a development proposal and land plan for a site that in your opinion should not be developed due to environmental limitations, including wetlands, floodplains, prime agricultural land, and soils unsuitable for septic tank drain fields. You also know that both the local government jurisdiction and the state are rather lax when it comes to enforcement of environmental regulations. What do you do? Should you take the assignment? (Carolin, Gerhart-Fritz, and Weitz 2012)

Commentary

It is clear from the AICP Code that you are obligated to give the client adequate and accurate information about the environmental limitations of the site and to share your opinion that it should not be developed (1). Further, it would not be appropriate for you to withhold information about the environmental limitations of the land proposed for development, because you should aspire to protect the environment (1.g).

If a planner believes that any development on the environmentally sensitive site would be contrary to the public interest, he or she should choose not to take the assignment. However, consultants are always aware that failure to serve a client's needs could lead that client to go elsewhere for the same services.

Other provisions of the AICP Code suggest implicitly that you need to go further with the analysis before deciding whether to take this assignment. For instance, principle 3.e suggests that without undertaking further analysis you should not accept customary solutions unless they fit the actual context. Is there some uncustomary land-development design that could fit on the environmentally sensitive site without causing long-term damage to the environment? Could innovative techniques be employed toward that end? After all, planners aspire to pursue excellence of design (1.g), and that aspiration could presumably be weighted equally with environmental protection since the principles are not ranked or prioritized in the AICP code.

The observations in the scenario that local and state environmental enforcement is lax should not hold any sway in the ethical decision-making process. If you accept the assignment with the suggestion or understanding that local and state laws and rules will not have to be fully complied with, you will most likely be in violation of rule of conduct 2, since you would at least be tacitly suggesting that compliance with laws and rules is not important.

Another consideration is your past public track record with any similar situations. If you have publicly advocated

Relevant AICP Code Provisions

Principles to Which We Aspire

1.g. Excellent design; preserve heritage

3.e. Apply customary solutions with caution

Rules of Conduct

1. Inaccurate information—untruthfulness
2. Illegal or unethical conduct
3. Change of public position on an issue

environmental protection at all costs and then plan a land development on a site that you believe for environmental reasons should not be developed, you open yourself up to a charge of violating rule of conduct 3.

After viewing all applicable code provisions, here is how I would proceed: Before speaking to the client, I would complete a preliminary examination of land-development practices that minimize environmental impact to assess their applicability on the subject site. I would also examine my own track record of public recommendations, with an eye toward spotting any inconsistencies between recommending development of the subject site and my past recommendations to other clients. If I had consistently and publicly recommended against development in similar circumstances, this would be determinative, as I would not want to violate rule 3.

If, in conducting the preliminary analysis of environmentally sensitive land practices applicable to the subject site, I concluded that some techniques could be acceptable—although they were costly and would mean that only minimal development could take place on the site—I would communicate that to the client. I would take the assignment, but only with the client's understanding that the scale and design of environmentally sensitive development I proposed may not meet her development goals and may prove too costly to implement. If the developer accepted these contingencies, I would prepare a land plan. If I still felt the site would be better left undeveloped, I would recommend that it not be developed and respectfully decline the assignment, knowing that the client may find another land planner to plan the site and that I may have lost the client for good. That is the unfortunate price the ethical planning practitioner will sometimes pay for acting in accordance with the AICP Code.

5

Community Development Block Grant Program Project Work Scope

You are the director of planning and community development in a community development block grant (CDBG) entitlement city. You have considerable discretion to propose a work scope that fits the goals and objectives of the city's consolidated plan for community development and responds to needs in the city. Your professional opinion, not yet publicly articulated, is that the funds should be used for low-income housing to benefit disadvantaged minority households, consistent with the consolidated plan. However, the city manager has informed you that the elected city council member who serves as liaison to the public works department (and who chairs the city council committee that has jurisdiction over this issue) wants to use the CDBG entitlement funds to upgrade water lines. How do you proceed in light of these differences in preferences?

Commentary

This scenario requires a multifaceted discussion, because it involves a policy issue, rather than misconduct—or, at least, misconduct has not yet surfaced. The most important question is how the community prefers to spend the CDBG program funds. What the elected council member—individually, not speaking for the whole council but as chair of a committee of the city council—wants to do with the funds should certainly be noted and considered. But more important, the consolidated plan is supposed to guide overall use of program funds, because it is an expression of policy and the desires of the community. It is appropriate for you to recommend the funds be allocated to a use that is suggested in the adopted consolidated plan: low-income housing. You are exercising independent professional judgment (2.a) in the matter to bring forth that recommendation. That independent judgment should continue to be preserved, regardless of the views of the council member who wants the funds to be used for water lines. The ethical issue is: How far do you go if a confrontation over this policy issue surfaces?

In anticipation of such a policy conflict, should you try to mobilize public support from disadvantaged persons in the community who need low-income housing? Is the upcoming public hearing enough to help council as a whole decide this issue, or is more meaningful participation needed (1.e)? Would mobilizing support for the consolidated plan's recommendation be within the bounds of your employer's expectations? Does the council member believe that you should acquiesce to his preferences (2.b)? Do you believe the public interest requires you to participate actively in the political process in an effort to execute the plan's recommendations, which are consistent with principle 1.f? To be ethical, shouldn't you "urge the alteration of policies, institutions, and decisions that oppose such needs" (1.f)? Are you required to prevent or at least voice disagreement to a decision that would oppose such needs?

Relevant AICP Code Provisions

Principles to Which We Aspire

1.e. Participation—meaningful impact

1.f. Social justice—plan for disadvantaged

1.h. Deal fairly and evenhandedly

2.a. Exercise independent judgment

2.b. Accept client decision unless illegal . . .

I would give the council a memo that reiterated the plan recommendation to use the funds for low-income housing and stated that I agreed with the adopted plan recommendation. In that memo, I would at least acknowledge the proposal by the council member to use the funds for water-line upgrades. If there was enough time, I would evaluate the water-line upgrade project for consistency with other goals and objectives of the consolidated plan.

I would consider sending out more than just standard notice of the public hearing to groups I knew would benefit from the low-income housing program. I would not necessarily do this in an attempt to mobilize people against the council member's idea, but rather to support what I viewed the public interest to be: the use of funds for low-income housing, which is a purpose identified in the consolidated plan. But then consider principle 1.h: "We shall deal fairly with all participants in the planning process. Those of us who are public officials or employees shall also deal evenhandedly with all planning process participants." If I singled out one client group for special notice and didn't extend it to all potential clients, would I violate 1.h? It seems only fair that any special notice be distributed to all potential client groups, not just the low-income groups I expected to support my view and the recommendations of the plan. Not to do so would violate that aspirational principle.

From there, I would let the process play its course without any additional extracurricular action. Closet politician planners (Howe 1994) might take more license than I would in this matter, maybe even working covertly on multiple fronts to win the policy battle. In my view, they begin to stretch the limits of a planner's autonomy to advocate his or her version of the public interest. And, after all, upgrading water lines still benefits the low-income community, because by CDBG program rules, the use must benefit low- and moderate-income populations. It would be appropriate to accept whatever decision the city council makes after the public hearing and council procedural deliberations in accordance with CDBG program requirements.

SCENARIO

6

Politically Influenced Population Projections 1

You are the planner in charge of producing a city's comprehensive plan, including population projections. You supplied a draft set of population projections showing that after the next decade the city will become "majority minority"—that is, more than 50 percent of the future population will be comprised of minorities. The mayor, who is white, does not like the implications of the race-specific projections and directs you to change them or cut them out of the draft comprehensive plan. How do you respond? (Based on Marcuse 1976)

Commentary

An initial issue is: Must you accept the mayor's directive as a "decision of the client" (2.b)? No, not in my view. The mayor has an important voice, but she does not necessarily speak for the elected city council as a whole in this instance. If the directive came from the city council as a whole, principle 2.b would likely influence my own decision.

Rule of conduct 9 appears to be relevant. It reads: "We shall not engage in private discussions with decision makers in the planning process in any manner prohibited by law or by agency rules, procedures, or custom." The mayor spoke with you privately about the draft comprehensive plan, and you are in the midst of a "planning process." I would research applicable laws, rules, and procedures to see if such private communication would constitute a violation. Even if there are no such violations, I would interpret rule 9 to apply to this context, because it is customary for many local governments that discussions with decision makers about plans and policies will occur in a public (not private) forum. From the scenario, it doesn't appear that you had a "discussion" with the mayor; you apparently just listened and have not yet responded. But if you engaged in an out-of-the-ordinary private discussion with the mayor, you would appear to be in violation of rule 9. A planner could politely inform the mayor that any discussion with a decision maker about the draft comprehensive plan in a "private" setting is outside or beyond what you believe is the customary conduit for elected officials to comment on the comprehensive plan draft, and that therefore you would likely violate rule 9 if you discussed the matter privately.

The mayor has given you two choices (should you choose to accept one of them): Change the projections or delete them. Note that it is the race-specific projection that is objectionable to the mayor, so you need not change or delete the projections of total population, which are essential to the planning process. Changing your work due to political pressure would be inappropriate, because planners should aspire to exercise independent professional judgment (2.a).

Relevant AICP Code Provisions

Principles to Which We Aspire

2.a. Exercise independent judgment
2.b. Accept client decision unless illegal . . .

Rules of Conduct

1. Inaccurate information— untruthfulness
9. Private communication (other)
19. Concealment of interest/failure to disclose

It is prudent to examine the applicability of rule of conduct 1, which reads: "We shall not deliberately or with reckless indifference fail to provide adequate, timely, clear and accurate information on planning issues." Projections cannot be evaluated with regard to adequacy or accuracy, since they pertain to a future condition which cannot be validated in the present state. On the other hand, if you accept the mayor's directive and delete the race-specific projections, are you deliberately failing to provide information on planning issues in violation of rule 1? In my view, no, because race-specific projections would not seem to have a major influence on a planning issue. There doesn't seem to be any violation of rules if you remove the race-specific projections from the draft, so I would remove them from the plan, keeping the total population projections as essential to the plan. Neither the integrity of the profession nor the planner's independent judgment is compromised significantly as a result of taking that action, in my view.

For Further Discussion

What about rule of conduct 19? Is it applicable? Rule 19 reads: "We shall not fail to disclose the interests of our client or employer when participating in the planning process. Nor shall we participate in an effort to conceal the true interests of our client or employer." While it is prudent to examine all rules as potentially applicable, I don't see a direct connection between this scenario and rule 19.

Minority Planner Acts as Advocate for Minority Neighborhood

A junior-level African American planner began work for a city that was completing a specific area plan covering an area including a low-income minority neighborhood. After reading the draft planning document, he formed an opinion that it was terrible and not in the best interest of the neighborhood. He informed his superiors of major concerns about the draft and lobbied them to make significant changes to it. He was told by the assistant planning director not to rock the boat by trying to make changes to the plan at that point. He then worked as an underground advocate for changes to the plan, without the knowledge of his supervisors. The city planning supervisors became aware of his activities. What ethical issues does this case raise? What should the junior-level planner do, and what action should the planning department managers take in response to his activities? (Based on Finkler 1971)

Commentary

There do not appear to be any rules of conduct that address this scenario directly. The junior planner has not been directed by his employer—that is, his supervisor—to work with the minority neighborhood to change the draft specific area plan. To the contrary, the assistant planning director has told the junior planner not to rock the boat. The junior planner should accept the decision of his supervisor as client unless the constraints his supervisor has placed on him are inconsistent with his conception of the public interest (2.b).

The junior planner can craft and articulate an argument that he should act under principle 1.f to urge changes to what he views as a terrible draft plan. We don't know the reasons for the junior planner's discontent about the draft plan, but we should assume they are valid from his viewpoint. There is room under principles 1.f and 2.a to arguably justify the junior planner going underground and actively working with the minority neighborhood in defiance of his employer's directive if the junior planner's conception of the public interest so dictates. However, in my view, that is not advisable, because the junior planner could be jeopardizing his status in the planning department. Should he lose the confidence of his managers, he will be even less effective at pursuing his conception of the public interest.

Because the junior planner is a young minority professional, the planning department managers should aspire under 3.f and 3.g to help him develop and advance professionally. If planning managers take extra time to work with the junior planner on this issue, it might help convince the junior planner that he will have more and better opportunities to make a difference in the community.

Relevant AICP Code Provisions

Principles to Which We Aspire

1.f. Social justice—plan for disadvantaged

2.a. Exercise independent judgment

2.b. Accept client decision unless illegal . . .

3.f. Contribute to professional development

3.g. Increase opportunity for underrepresented groups

Planners Oppose Their Own Department Director at Public Hearing

A group of three planners working for a large city planning department are opposed to the rezoning of a block in the city's downtown for luxury apartment buildings, because they are concerned that it will displace low- and moderate-income residents from the block and neighborhood. They made their concerns known to the planning director, who is an AICP member, but the planning director overruled them and recommended approval of the rezoning. At the planning commission, the three planners appeared and testified against the rezoning, also adding that the planning director, who is their boss, had capitulated to the real estate industry in overriding the recommendations of her own staff. Is this a legitimate case for the three planners or the planning director to complain about an AICP Code infraction? (Based on Finkler 1971)

Commentary

Principles of the AICP Code might serve as defenses for the three planners in their action. They were exercising their independent judgment (2.a) in not accepting the planning director's recommendation, because it violated their conception of the public interest (2.b). The three planners could also argue they aspire to achieve social justice and to urge alterations of decisions (including the director's recommendations) that are damaging to the interests of the disadvantaged (1.f).

Another possible defense of the three planners might be rule of conduct 19. Under that rule, the planners have a duty to disclose the interests of their client or employer; and, in this case, the disadvantaged, in addition to the city, could be considered the client. According to rule 19, the planners are also duty bound to disclose, not conceal, the true interests of their employer, as expressed by the planning director; and, in their view, her interests were purely the interests of the real estate industry.

An argument based only on aspirations and a weak reference to one rule of conduct cannot stand up to multiple adverse applicable rules of conduct. The planning director would be right to object to the three planners' testimony before the city on several grounds. First, it was not fair and professional of them to level allegations of collusion with the real estate industry for the first time in a public forum, thus making their action contrary to principle 3.c. Second, although we cannot judge the veracity of the three planners' charges against the planning director, rule of conduct 10 provides that we shall not deliberately or with reckless indifference misrepresent the views of other professionals—the planning director, in this case. There is room for error and misconduct in that regard if charges are untrue or misleading or leveled with malicious intent. Also, while it may be a stretch of the strict construction of the AICP Code, are the three planners

Relevant AICP Code Provisions

Principles to Which We Aspire

1.f. Social justice—plan for disadvantaged
2.a. Exercise independent judgment
2.b. Accept client decision unless illegal . . .
3.c. Treat other professionals fairly

Rules of Conduct

10. Misrepresentation of others' qualifications
18. Pressure: unsubstantiated findings
19. Concealment of interest/failure to disclose
24. No frivolous ethics charge

attempting to coax the director to reach findings and con-clusions that she doesn't believe are supported by available evidence (18)? And, finally, although rule of conduct 24 is likely limited in context to "charges of ethical misconduct," if proved wrong, wouldn't the three planners have violated this rule by frivolously charging ethical misconduct?

It seems that the three planners' charges of misconduct on the part of the planning director have no immediate merit. On the other hand, they may have set themselves up to be ac-cused of violating multiple rules of conduct of the AICP Code.

Recommendation for Housing Trust Fund Disapproved by Board

You are the executive director of a nonprofit housing agency, answerable to an appointed board of directors. In the annual work program, which you initiate, you recommend the establishment of a housing trust fund targeted at low- and moderate-income households in the jurisdiction served by the agency. Although you make carefully reasoned arguments in writing to the board in support of your recommendation, the board votes not to include the housing trust fund for execution in the annual work program. You feel strongly about the need for the trust fund. What do you do?

Commentary

This is a confrontation between the need to be accountable and the desire to be loyal to your employer, and the need to independently pursue the planner's notion of the public interest, which, according to the AICP Code, is constantly evolving and is also described to some extent by the aspirational principles of the code (listed in box at right).

Do you feel so strongly about this that you are thinking of finding some other way to get the housing trust fund initiated? Would you do that through your employer or through some other means?

My sense is that you should accept, if not respect, the agency board's decision to exclude the housing trust fund from the work program. However, if you are aware of other means besides your agency that might accomplish the same objective, you are justified in continuing discussions with the client group about how to best effectuate the housing trust fund without the agency's direct involvement.

Relevant AICP Code Provisions

Principles to Which We Aspire

1.e. Participation—meaningful impact
1.f. Social justice—plan for disadvantaged
2.a. Exercise independent judgment
2.b. Accept client decision unless illegal . . .
3.j. Contribute to those lacking resources

10 County Jail Proposal in City Center Neighborhood

You are a county planning director, and the county you work for is pushing to build a new jail in a mostly industrial area of a central city within your county. You are friends with the planners in the city, who have copied you on their detailed report opposing the jail project. On a weekly basis, you read the local newspaper, which has reported that the city is opposed to the county placing a new jail there. You get called into a meeting with the county sheriff, chair of the board of county commissioners, and the county administrator. Although they don't need any authority from the city to site the jail in the proposed location, in an effort to counter the city's report they ask that your office prepare a site selection study demonstrating community need and also showing the appropriateness of the jail at the proposed location. You politely indicate that you don't support the jail project, as it is counter to numerous planning goals in the city's comprehensive plan and redevelopment plan. The meeting ends, and the next day you learn from the assistant county administrator that the county has hired a private consultant to write the report desired by the county officials. In just a few more days, the newspaper reports that the county-financed private consultant has released a report supporting the jail location. You obtain and read the consultant's report, authored by an AICP certified planner. You think the report is terribly sloppy and inept. Further, you consider it unethical for an AICP planner to have written the report in such a short period of time. You strongly believe the consultant put the report together based exclusively on the county's desire to support the jail project, to the clear neglect of technical information that other planners would surely consider in drafting report recommendations. How do you handle this situation?

Commentary

I would examine the consultant's report in light of the AICP Code Rules of Conduct. The consultant may have failed to provide accurate and adequate information about the county's proposed jail and its impacts on the city center, thus potentially violating rule 1. In addition, the consultant may have violated rule of conduct 16 by accepting an assignment that could not be performed as promptly as it was completed under the complex circumstances.

If I could document severe errors of information in the consultant's report, I would pursue an ethics complaint against the consultant, taking proper care to treat the professional fairly (3.c). A second possible action, again assuming documentation of erroneous information in the consultant's report, is to publicly release information that discredits and corrects the consultant's report. If I took this second action, it would involve great risk: County officials are likely to get perturbed. The officials seemed to accept the refusal to write the report in the first place, but if I undermined the county's investment in the consultant's report, that action could be received by county leaders as me refusing to accept my employer's decision in the matter (contrary to 2.b). Nonetheless, if I knew the consultant's report was erroneous, I would be obligated under rule 1 to "provide adequate, timely, clear and accurate information," presuming

Relevant AICP Code Provisions

Principles to Which We Aspire

1.d. Provide information to all affected

2.a. Exercise independent judgment

2.b. Accept client decision unless illegal...

3.c. Treat other professionals fairly

Rules of Conduct

1. Inaccurate information— untruthfulness

16. Promptness of work required

the jail siting was a "planning issue." In this case there is a conflict between a rule of conduct and a principle; the rule of conduct must prevail since the rule of conduct is enforceable. Also supporting this second action are the principles of exercising independent judgment (2.a) and providing information to all those affected and to decision makers (1.d).

SCENARIO

11

University Professor Subcontracts for Work Involving State or University Funds

You are a university professor and also have your own planning consulting firm. You have permission according to personnel rules—that is, the faculty manual—to do consulting work when it does not conflict with your primary duties at the university. An outreach branch of the university has received money from the state to pay for a local government planning project and has hired a local consulting firm to complete the project. The manager of the consulting firm approaches you and asks if you will prepare a portion of the planning project report for pay under subcontract. How do you respond? Can you accept the assignment, and if so, under what circumstances?

Commentary

You owe diligent and competent work to the university (2, preamble). You should not do additional work if it would take away from your ability to meet the obligations of your primary employer. Because permission to consult is stated in writing in the faculty manual, if you disclose the consulting work to the university as required, you have met the obligations of rule of conduct 4.

However, the situation has the appearance of a conflict of interest: It may be perceived by an inquiring public as a covert kickback mechanism. In this scenario, state money is given to the university outreach branch to pay for a service or product. The outreach branch has constraints but also some discretion to: (1) arrange for the university faculty to complete planning projects or (2) award the money to a local government grant recipient, which may then hire a consulting firm, with or without the involvement and recommendation of the outreach branch. The state funds given to the university outreach branch can then be channeled to its own faculty, through arrangements and agreements, to enable the completion of the project.

However, the indirect nature of the conduit for the flow of funds has to be critically examined. In this scenario, a secondary conduit is established for paying you, and you benefit from the state funds as a private consultant. Such an arrangement is outside the context of the university's norms and expectations; therefore, you are obligated to disclose your involvement and seek permission. If you provide disclosure and gain permission from the university with the consent of the outreach branch, you can take on and complete the assignment, even though you will receive payment through your consulting firm rather than as extra pay through the university.

Relevant AICP Code Provisions

Principles to Which We Aspire

2. (preamble) Competent performance
2.c. Avoid appearance of conflict of interest

Rules of Conduct

4. Outside employment ("moonlighting")
14. Official power used for advantage

For Further Discussion

Does it make a difference if you had solicited this work, as opposed to being approached by another consulting firm with a contract in hand? Could solicitation of the work be considered a violation of rule 14, because you would be using the power of your position as university professor to seek or obtain a special advantage—that is, a private consulting contract? Do your conclusions change if the arrangement is not a matter of public knowledge?

12 Junior Planner Assists Development Applicant

You are the planning manager for a local government. You and your staff are responsible for preparing a written recommendation for a rezoning application on the next agenda of the planning commission. You assigned a junior planner, who is not an AICP member, to write the recommendation. She submitted to you a draft staff report recommending approval. In looking at the sketch plan and zoning exhibit for the rezoning application, you notice that something about them looks very familiar. Then it clicks: You have seen the style and content of the drawing before, and you are certain that the site plan was drawn by the junior planner who wrote the report and recommendation. You also now recall that the junior planner seemed to be quite friendly with the rezoning applicant in past visits to the office. What do you do?

Commentary

You should first consult the local government's personnel regulations and any applicable state laws regarding the employee's activities, because the planner is not an AICP member and therefore is not subject to enforcement of violations of any rules of misconduct. Although the AICP Code does not apply in the case of an infraction by the junior planner, she is still supposed to follow the APA ethical principles. For instance, the principles indicate that planners cannot accept gifts, favors, or advantage intended or expected to influence a planner's decision-making objectivity. It has not been proven in this scenario that the junior planner was paid for the work or did it as a favor to a friend, but if that is the case, she is unlikely to maintain impartiality.

If you suspect the junior planner prepared the site plan and assisted the development applicant, you should obtain some proof of it. You could ask the planner if she prepared the site plan. Or you could search for another site plan or product prepared by the junior planner for local government work and compare it to the site plan submitted with the application, checking further for similarities in content and drawing style. If the junior planner admits she assisted the development applicant, or additional proof is found indicating that she did, the junior planner should be disciplined according to applicable local personnel rules. Even if local personnel regulations do not specifically require the junior planner to seek permission to consult (rule 4) or do not otherwise disallow the junior planner's activity, she is a planner and must act with integrity, as is expected of all planning professionals.

If the junior planner offered services for a fee and indicated she could also influence the planning staff's recommendation on the rezoning application, she would (if an AICP member) be in violation of rule of conduct 11. She has violated the public trust by compromising public authority for private gain

Relevant AICP Code Provisions

Principles to Which We Aspire

3.f. Contribute to professional development

Rules of Conduct

4. Outside employment ("moonlighting")
11. Solicitation via false claims; duress
25. Deliberate, wrongful act

or to extend help to a friend. For an AICP member, this would also violate rule of conduct 25.

Whether you, the planning manager, hold the AICP credential or not, it would be advisable for you to recognize that the junior planner is a young professional and that aspirational principles of the AICP Code, as well as the APA ethical principles in planning, suggest we contribute time and resources to the professional development of beginning professionals (3.f). Such professional development includes ethics training. Hence, if the junior planner learns that she made a mistake, progress has been made.

SCENARIO

13 Potential Conflict With Public and Nonprofit Roles

You are the planning director for a local government and have been asked to join the board of directors of a nonprofit organization that seeks to create more affordable housing in the region. If you serve in a leadership role for the nonprofit organization, might those responsibilities cause an ethical conflict with your responsibilities as planning director? (Derived from Perego 2008)

Commentary

As this long list of code provisions illustrates, this seemingly innocuous proposal raises numerous ethical issues upon close, systematic examination of the AICP Code. The nonprofit organization is pursuing goals that are highly consistent with core values in the AICP Code, so playing a role in the nonprofit organization could allow you to satisfy several of the code's aspirational principles. The regional nonprofit organization is an excellent fit, enabling you to bring about achievements that may be more difficult to accomplish as a local government employee. Everything seems to point to you accepting the appointment.

Not so fast! There are many other considerations. An appointment of a local government employee to the board of a regional nonprofit organization might or might not be considered "employment." Regardless, the appointment would raise the prospect of a conflict of interest (2.c) between your duties in your position as local government planning director and the obligations of service to the nonprofit group. The nonprofit group has many stakeholders, so acceptance of the board appointment involves additional dimensions of public interest and allegiances with numerous client groups. The goals and objectives of the client groups, as expressed through the nonprofit board, could conflict with the policies of your employer, the local government. For instance, the board may undertake activities in your local jurisdiction, which may not be receptive to that type of development within its boundaries. Also, there may be pressure for you to disclose privileged local government information (rule 7).

Per rule of conduct 4, you should gain written permission from your employer to serve on the regional nonprofit board. You should do so even if you conclude that the board appointment is not legally interpreted as "employment" as referenced in rule 4. In addition to securing local government approval to serve on the nonprofit board, it is advisable for you to set in writing some parameters and contingencies of your nonprofit board service that protect the interests of the local government and address how any reasonably anticipated situations of conflict of interest will be resolved (2.c). There are a number of

Relevant AICP Code Provisions

Principles to Which We Aspire

1.f. Social justice—plan for disadvantaged
2. (preamble) Competent performance
2.c. Avoid appearance of conflict of interest
3 (preamble) Contribute to profession
3.b. Educate public on planning issues
3.j. Contribute to those lacking resources

Rules of Conduct

4. Outside employment ("moonlighting")
7. Breach of confidentiality

serious potential mishaps and ethical problems that could easily arise and which you should contemplate prior to accepting the nonprofit board appointment. Planners can also consider preparing and seeking approval of a conflict-of-interest management plan; such a document could specify in advance what constitutes a conflict of interest and certain actions you will take if a conflict of interest arises. Your employer's acceptance of such a plan can protect you from the worst potential transgressions.

14 Investment Opportunity in Jurisdiction of Work

You are a county planner and have the opportunity to invest in a corporation that is developing assisted living centers. At least one of the sites proposed for an assisted living center is within the county where you work. As a passive investor, you will play no active role in business operations; a team of consultants will handle all aspects of the development and approval processes and, when the centers are completed, a service provider will be hired to operate and administer them. Is this investment wise from an ethical perspective? (Derived from Perego 2008)

Commentary

Having a monetary stake in a company that is doing work in the county where you work as a planner may create an appearance of a conflict of interest contrary to 2.c of the code. Rule of conduct 4 is also worth examining closely. Is an investment opportunity of the sort described in this scenario considered "employment"? Probably not. And is real estate development a "related profession" to planning? A strict constructionist of the code could argue that it is not. Do you have a right to invest your own dollars in any investment scheme that is legal? Perhaps you do. However, is it enough to simply ask these questions?

The safe play, in the spirit of rule 4, is to seek the approval of the local government to engage in the investment opportunity. I would disclose my investment intentions and seek the local government's approval even if persuasive arguments can be made that this is not employment in a related profession. If the local government balks at the idea, I would find another investment opportunity more in line with my obligations as a public-sector planner. The ethical planning practitioner will also critically analyze the potential conflicts further.

Relevant AICP Code Provisions

Principles to Which We Aspire

2.c. Avoid appearance of conflict of interest

Rules of Conduct

4. Outside employment ("moonlighting")

15 Planning Consultant Considers Planning Commission Appointment

You are a consulting planner who specializes in land use and entitlements for private landowners in a city where you also reside. You are interested in applying for an upcoming vacancy on the planning commission for the same jurisdiction. You discuss the prospect with the city's planning director, who conveys the opinion that you should not conduct any more business in the city if you are appointed to the city planning commission, as it may be a conflict of interest. You believe you can recuse yourself if there is a direct conflict of interest. Who is right? Do you need to cease all business in the city if you are going to serve on the city planning commission? (Carolin, Gerhart-Fritz, and Weitz 2012)

Commentary

There is significant wisdom in the opinion of the city's planning director. As the long list of rule provisions indicates, there is much potential for things to go awry if you accept the appointment to the planning commission and continue to do business in the city. There are also aspirational principles that could come into play, but given that so many rules of conduct potentially apply, I have not listed all of them.

Because of your planning commission appointment, you might gain additional consulting clients. If new clients hired you because of potential or implied influence in swaying the city's decisions on development matters, you would appear to violate rule of conduct 5, which prohibits receiving advantage on the basis of a public position. As a planning commissioner, you would be a public official. Others, such as competing planning consultants, might perceive that you have a special advantage with future development entitlement applicants as a result of your planning commission appointment. It would not be in the public interest for you to use the appointment as planning commissioner to obtain any special advantage (14), and an edge over other planning consultants in gaining clients would be a special advantage if it accrued as a result of the planning commission appointment. You would also violate rule of conduct 13 if, in attempting to gain work, you suggested to a prospective client that because you served on the planning commission you thus had some extracurricular influence.

The dual roles of planning consultant and planning commissioner would be a conflict of interest (2.c) in a case where you attempted to bring forth an application of one of your private-sector clients and participated in any way in the deliberations of the planning commission on that matter. In such an instance, you would certainly be correct in recusing yourself; it would be prudent if not required. It would seem that you could use recusal as often as necessary to avoid direct conflicts or the

Relevant AICP Code Provisions

Principles to Which We Aspire

2.c. Avoid appearance of conflict of interestt

Rules of Conduct

3. Change of public position on an issue
5. Acceptance of gifts or advantage
8. Private communication (public)
9. Private communication (other)
13. Influence via improper means
14. Official power used for advantage
19. Concealment of interest/ failure to disclose

perception of conflicts between impartial deliberations in your role as planning commissioner and in your role as advocate for your private clients' developments. But conflicts between the interest of the city and your private development clients could surface in a number of other important ways. It may be difficult for you, acting as planner and planning commissioner, not to violate rule of conduct 19. That rule obliges planners who are AICP members to "disclose the interests of our client or employer when participating in the planning process"—meaning, in this case, the city as client and the developer as client. Further, in rule 19, planners are required to be truthful and shall not "conceal the true interests of our client or employer." Taken literally, this obligation could put the planner in some undesirable situations. And rule of conduct 3 is a good example of this potential minefield: By taking on more development clients, the prospects increase that you would be publicly advocating a position different from those you would publicly take as a member of the city planning commission. There is also the potential for inappropriate communications as a result of working in both capacities (rules 8 and 9).

Given all of this, seeking the appointment appears too dangerous from an ethics standpoint, and the advice of the city planning director should prevail. However, with that said, it is worth mentioning your apparent desire to give back to the community by serving as a volunteer, which is consistent with certain aspirational principles in the AICP Code. And it seems unnecessarily harsh for you to have to cease all activities involving development clients in the jurisdiction where you are serving as planning commissioner; after all, your work in the city appears to be your livelihood and the area where your expertise helps most with client recruitment. If the potential conflicts can all be anticipated and written up in a conflict-of-interest management plan, there may be ways to serve on the planning commission while still doing business for clients in the city. However, in my view, the potential for multiple conflicts over time is too likely to condone the dual roles. Multiple recusals due to your private clients would not reflect well on your integrity or the integrity of the planning profession.

16   Public and Private Client Conflict

You are a consulting planner under contract to prepare a zoning ordinance for a city, and you were on the city government planning staff a short time earlier. A developer has approached you and is intent on eventually upzoning a large parcel of land in the jurisdiction for which you are preparing the new zoning ordinance. The developer asks you if you will take the developer on as a client and provide "political" advice about individual council members and how to proceed with getting the property upzoned. What can you do? (Carolin, Gerhart-Fritz, and Weitz 2012)

Commentary

If the situation is a conflict of interest, then 2.c implies that you should not engage in the work. Some of the rules cited are on the fringes of applicability, but their intent should be considered relevant nonetheless. There is a lot of room for you to get into trouble with rule of conduct 3, if you take public positions that are inconsistent with your prior positions. Rule 4 may not be technically applicable, because you are a "contracted" rather than "salaried" employee, but it is instructive and could still be considered applicable in terms of its overall intent to require you to disclose other employment and to get prior permission (also evident in rule 3). It may be argued that rule of conduct 6 is inapplicable to this scenario, but one can observe that this consulting assignment arises as a direct result of your prior status as the city's planning director: Your advice is sought by the developer purely because of what you learned and know about the politics of the city. And if applicable, rule 6 would require disclosure by you and permission from the employer before you work for the developer, since the city is already your client. Hence, three rules point to the need for disclosure and prior permission in order to proceed.

Someone could observe that you open yourself up to a potential violation of rule of conduct 7, regarding the leaking of confidential city information to the developer. If you solicited this work with the developer and in any way suggested or implied an ability to influence the city's code-writing process, and those suggestions were false or misleading, you would be guilty of violating rules 11 and 13. If a relationship exists between you and the developer when it comes time for the city to consider the proposed new zoning ordinance, wouldn't you have to disclose your interest (paid work) and the interests of the developer, because the developer is a client? If you did not, wouldn't you violate rule of conduct 19? And if such public disclosure were given, would that be an act that reflects adversely on our professional fitness, thus violating rule 25? These questions should lead the ethical planning practitioner to avoid situations of this sort in the first place.

Relevant AICP Code Provisions

Principles to Which We Aspire

2.c. Avoid appearance of conflict of interest

Rules of Conduct

2. Illegal or unethical conduct
3. Change of public position on an issue
4. Outside employment ("moon-lighting")
6. Personal or financial gain
7. Breach of confidentiality
11. Solicitation via false claims; duress
13. Influence via improper means
19. Concealment of interest/failure to disclose
25. Deliberate, wrongful act

17 Public Planner Connects With Development Community on LinkedIn

You are a planner employed by a county government, and you are assigned primarily to writing staff reports for rezoning proposals and reviewing site plans for land development permits. In the course of your work you have interacted with numerous other professionals. You are a member of LinkedIn (a professional network), which identifies you as a county planner, and you are interested in expanding your connections. Your connections are available for viewing by the public. You receive invitations to connect on LinkedIn from the managing partner of a real estate development firm, a land-use attorney who frequently represents rezoning applicants in the county, and a civil engineer for a firm that commonly prepares land development plans for property owners and developers in the county. You have worked with all of these professionals as county planner, so you accept them as connections. Are there any ethical implications or issues associated with accepting these invitations to connect?

Commentary

If the public sees that you are "connected" with development applicants and other private interests, could that be inconsistent with principle 2.c? What does it mean to be "connected" (Salkin and Tappendorf 2011)? Is a connection interpreted simply as someone you know and have some general association with, or does it imply something more than a casual acquaintance? People's perceptions of what your connections mean can clearly differ. And motivations by professionals to accept other professionals as a LinkedIn connection will also vary considerably. Any member of the inquiring public could conceivably raise an eyebrow about your relationship with other professionals with whom you are connected on LinkedIn.

This ethics scenario is a good example of why planners need to read the entire principle and not rely exclusively on any generalized paraphrasing of the principle, such as that provided in Table 1. Per the full wording of principle 2.c, planners need to avoid the appearance of a conflict of interest "in accepting assignments from clients or employers." A LinkedIn connection has nothing to do with an assignment from your employer, and therefore there should be no violation of principle 2.c to have such connections. If you choose to be connected with individuals with whom you have worked, that would seem to be appropriate given the general purposes of LinkedIn. While a question about your relationship with someone with whom you are associated could be raised by anyone, there is certainly nothing by virtue of a connection in LinkedIn that could be explicitly interpreted as a conflict of interest in any work you have been assigned by the county as your employer, and little if anything inherent in a given connection to suggest an appearance of a conflict of interest, since the connection relationship is disassociated with any

Relevant AICP Code Provisions

Principles to Which We Aspire

2.c. Avoid appearance of conflict of interest

Rules of Conduct

8. Private communication (public)
20. Unlawful discrimination

specific assignments given to you by your employer. Many planners will dismiss this as a nonissue, especially given that compliance with any principles to which we aspire in Section A of the AICP Code of Ethics cannot be enforced.

However, the ethical planner will consider the potential for an appearance of a conflict of interest outside the narrow context of the literal wording of a given principle. Furthermore, the ethical planner will contemplate how a connection with someone on LinkedIn could present opportunities for ethical mishaps. For example, consider rule of conduct 8, which reads "We shall not, as public officials or employees, engage in private communications with planning process participants if the discussions relate to a matter over which we have authority to make a binding, final determination if such private communications are prohibited by law or by agency rules, procedures, or custom." LinkedIn enables private communication. Therefore, it presents an opportunity for a development permit applicant to contact you privately regarding a land development project or other matter. Since you as a county planner presumably have authority to make a "binding, final determination" on plans submitted for a land development permit, a private communication via LinkedIn about a land development permit assigned to you for review could conceivably rise to the level of a violation of rule 8, if such private communication is prohibited by law or agency rules, procedures, or customs.

18 Consistency in Zoning Administration

You are the zoning administrator for a local government. Last month, you made an official administrative interpretation of the zoning ordinance that allowed a well-known, high-status developer to receive approval for construction of a building. Now you are confronted with a building proposal in virtually identical circumstances from a resident in a low-income, minority neighborhood, who faces the same zoning ordinance provision. How do you respond to the resident's building proposal?

Commentary

You should authorize issuance of the building permit. Who the applicant is should have no bearing on your decision. If the zoning ordinance interpretation is good for one person, it should be good for any other person, as long as the circumstances are identical or virtually the same. The ethical planner administers the zoning ordinance with objectivity, impartiality, and consistency. The integrity of the profession relies on it (3.a). If the circumstances are the same, both applicants should get approved for permits.

It would not be appropriate in this case to give favored treatment to one permittee and deny the same type of permit request of another on any basis except for the rules governing compliance with issuing permits. The low-income resident deserves the same decision as the more wealthy developer, who received the permit based on administrative discretion and interpretation. One could even say it is the "right" of the low-income resident to obtain permit approval under the circumstances (1.a).

Relevant AICP Code Provisions

Principles to Which We Aspire
1.a. Consider rights of others
3.a. Enhance professional integrity

19

Planning Consultant Buys Lunch for Public-Sector Clients

You are a planning consultant who has contracts with a county for comprehensive planning and with a state transportation agency for policy work. When you work on the county job, you frequently invite selected county staff members out to lunch, and you pay. When you offer to buy lunch for the state transportation planner, he declines. Is the state planner right to pay for his own lunch, and are the county planners wrong for accepting the free lunches? And should you quit offering to pay for lunches with clients?

Commentary
Respect the state agency planner's nonacceptance of your offer to pay for lunch, and don't ask again. If you desire, continue to offer lunch to the county planners, as it does not appear to violate any principles or rules of the AICP Code. Rule of conduct 11 comes closest: "We shall not solicit prospective clients or employment through use of false or misleading claims, harassment, or duress." In this scenario, you are not soliciting clients, because they are already your clients, but you could be tacitly courting future contracts with these existing clients. Even if you are (and what private businessperson would not always be courting future contracts?), buying lunch would not be considered a misleading claim, harassment, or duress. Hence, rule 11 doesn't apply.

For Further Discussion
Although the scenario focuses on your ethics as the consulting planner, one can ask questions about the ethical conduct of the county planners and the state agency planner, who hold public positions. Why does the state planner act differently from the county planners and not accept your offer to pay for lunch? The difference might be attributed to different perceptions of ethics, but it is more likely because the state planner is subject to an agency ruling, statewide code of conduct, or law relating to conflicts of interest that address this matter, while the county planners are not.

Relevant AICP Code Provisions

Rules of Conduct

11. Solicitation via false claims; duress

SCENARIO 20

Administrative Discretion: Recommending a Grant Recipient

You are a city planner who administers a competitive home ownership down-payment assistance program. You are charged with recommending to the city manager which applicants will be awarded the assistance. There are two applications for one award, and both applicants meet the minimum standards for receipt of the assistance. On various comparison factors, the two applicants are more or less equal. You choose one on the basis that she is a disadvantaged minority. Is this an appropriate recommendation?

Commentary

In my own view, the "planning process," as referenced in the AICP Code, should be interpreted broadly as any public decision-making process in which the planner is engaged. Principle 1.f of the code does not have to be read as an affirmative-action policy. However, there does not appear to be any direct provision of the AICP Code that prevents you from determining that it is more in the public interest to award the assistance to the disadvantaged minority than the other applicant because of principle 1.f.

I would probably deliver a report to the city manager stating that both applicants were equally qualified for the assistance, so the decision was a toss-up. I would verbalize to the city manager that in a case such as this, where applicants are equally qualified, I would make the decision in favor of the minority resident, given principle 1.f. But I would not criticize a planner who elected not to verbalize such a statement.

Relevant AICP Code Provisions

Principles to Which We Aspire

1.f. Social justice—plan for disadvantaged

Politically Influenced Population Projections 2

You are the planner in charge of producing a county's comprehensive plan, including population projections. You supplied a draft set of population projections showing that the county will begin losing population at the end of the decade and will continue to lose significant population during the 20-year planning horizon. After the meeting of the comprehensive plan steering committee, the executive director of the chamber of commerce pulls you aside and privately scolds you for not recognizing the adverse repercussions on future economic development that comes from publishing negative population projections, even in draft form. The executive director intimates that he will bring pressure down on you through elected officials and the county manager if the projections are not changed to show relatively stable population growth or only a modest decrease in population. How do you respond?

Commentary

The executive director of the chamber of commerce is not part of the county government proper and is therefore a stakeholder but not your employer or primary client. This scenario involves total county population projections, which are indispensable to every aspect of the comprehensive plan (1.d).

Your response might depend on how much of the comprehensive plan had already been prepared in reliance on those population projections. If it is already late in the process of plan development, changing the projections could cause a substantial unraveling of the internal consistency of the planning document and hence lead to a significant amount of work to revise other plan elements. If it is early in the process of plan development, where community facilities and land-use plans have not been carefully crafted in concert with those population projections, then you might placate the executive director by telling him you will take another look at the population projections. You could diplomatically explain that planners must exercise independent professional judgment (2.a) and that his suggestion is improper.

I would probably hold fast to the validity of the projections, leaving them unchanged. I would probably also write a polite memo to the executive director thanking him for the suggestion but explaining the reasons why I believe the projections are appropriate as presented. Planners have to be cognizant of the repercussions of backing down in the face of pressure from a stakeholder, however powerful he or she may be. If you do as the chamber's executive director wishes, the next time an issue of this sort manifests, he and perhaps other stakeholders may believe that you have no backbone and that, by applying pressure, they can influence your recommendations. That would set a bad precedent for maintaining integrity in the future. It would also be prudent to inform your boss and/or elected officials of what happened.

See the commentary under S6 for further discussion.

Relevant AICP Code Provisions

Principles to Which We Aspire

1.d. Provide information to all affected

2.a. Exercise independent judgment

SCENARIO 22
Consulting With Municipality Immediately After Quitting

A city planner decides to quit her public-sector job and take a position with a private planning firm. The consulting planner's first task is to respond to a request for proposal issued by the city that she just quit. Is this a conflict or ethical issue? (APA 2012)

Commentary

There do not appear to be any AICP Code provisions that directly relate to this scenario. After raising several questions about circumstances not evident in the scenario, APA (2012, p. 21) concludes that "often, the fact situation will be the determining factor when judging behavior under the code."

Relevant AICP Code Provisions

None

23 Contractual Requirements of State for Land-Use Planning Grant

You are a planner working for a state agency that distributes grants to local governments for land-use planning. A precondition of receiving a state grant is that the local government complies with certain state requirements. One of the local government recipients of a state planning grant you are assigned to administer is not meeting those requirements. You are conflicted about what to do, because if you insist on enforcement of the grant requirements, and the local government still does not comply, your only recourse will be to have the state agency cut the funding; in that case, you anticipate the local government will not complete the plan. What do you do? (Based on Howe 1994)

Commentary

This scenario appears to fall mostly outside the rules of conduct of the AICP Code. Rule of conduct 2, the only one I can identify as relevant, prohibits unlawful activity and suggests you should not participate in actions that would violate the state agency procedures, however codified. However, this scenario begs planners to consider whether the greater interest in good planning is an acceptable justification for the bending or ignoring of grant rules. Personally, I wouldn't go there. Even though it is for a good cause—that is, good planning—my view is that bending or ignoring the grant rules is inconsistent with ethical principles of the AICP Code. Planners should not elevate planning as an end if unethical means are used to accomplish it.

Relevant AICP Code Provisions

Rules of Conduct

2. Illegal or unethical conduct

24 Recommendations Regarding Nearly Identical Rezoning Requests

You are a planner who evaluates rezoning requests and makes rezoning recommendations for a medium-sized town. Six months ago, you had a case where you recommended denial of a rezoning request for a moderate-density residential subdivision at the suburbanizing fringe of the town. Your reasons for recommending denial were its inconsistency with the future land-use plan and the unavailability of sanitary sewer service, which was more than 2,000 feet away. Now you have another case that is virtually identical in characteristics. However, the applicant is a respected developer in the community, whom you have worked with in reviewing zoning applications for the city several times in the past three years. He has a track record of producing high-quality residential product within and outside of your jurisdiction. What do you recommend?

Commentary

For consistency, you should recommend denial. It should make no difference whether the applicant is an amateur developer or respected developer. Rule of conduct 3 (not cited as a relevant code provision) discusses consistency in determinations, but it doesn't apply in this case because it requires consistency between decisions made for an existing client and for former clients (1.h). Consistency is an important component of integrity. It is not fair to treat applicants with nearly identical circumstances differently.

Relevant AICP Code Provisions

Principles to Which We Aspire

1.h. Deal fairly and evenhandedly

25 Accessory Apartments Recommended as Affordable Housing

A planner is working on implementing more affordable housing programs for a city with a population of 20,000. In researching options, he posts on an email list server a question about other local government zoning provisions on the subject. A planner from another city, which has a population of 80,000, provides her city's accessory apartment ordinance provisions. The first planner, who has a challenging workload and wants to move on to the next planning issue, takes the provisions and, without additional research or thought, recommends them to his city's planning commission. Could this be considered ethical misconduct?

Commentary

The planning practitioner owes his client diligent performance of work (2, preamble). It is ill-advised for him to accept one local government's regulations and apply them blindly in another jurisdiction. Planners need to follow the principle that we will examine the applicability of solutions and not accept them unless they are reasonably applicable to the subject jurisdiction (3.e).

Relevant AICP Code Provisions

Principles to Which We Aspire

2.	(preamble) Competent performance

3.e.	Apply customary solutions with caution

SCENARIO 26

Disadvantaged Group Input

You are a planning consultant with a contract to prepare a plan for a county and also a separate contract to prepare a plan for a city in the same county. You find that the elected officials of the city are not inclined to seek input from a low-income, disadvantaged, mostly African American neighborhood. An opportunity arises for you to meet with residents of this neighborhood, and the meeting will be recorded and televised. You don't want to ask your city client if you should attend, because you believe the city is likely to say no. What do you do? (Based on Carolin, Gerhart-Fritz, and Weitz 2012)

Commentary

You should attend the session. This situation does not appear to involve any rules of conduct, but multiple ethical principles of the AICP Code apply. Residents of the low-income, disadvantaged, mostly African American neighborhood deserve the opportunity to have a meaningful impact in the planning process (1.e). Social justice also enters into the considerations (1.f). Educating and contributing time to groups is encouraged (3.b and 3.j). You should find a way to attend the scheduled gathering, provide information, and seek input.

For Further Discussion

Should you ask the city for permission to attend the gathering? What if you ask the city's permission and the city leaders decline, suggesting that it is not necessary? In light of the aspirational principles of the AICP Code, should you then exercise independent judgment (2.a) and attend the gathering anyway? Or would you then violate principle 2.b by not accepting the direction of the client? Is it ethical for you to contradict the directive of the client? Can you ignore the directive on the basis that you aspire to uphold the public interest and AICP Code principles?

Relevant AICP Code Provisions

Principles to Which We Aspire

1.e. Participation—meaningful impact

1.f. Social justice—plan for disadvantaged

2.a. Exercise independent judgment

2.b. Accept client decision unless illegal . . .

3.b. Educate public on planning issues

3.j. Contribute to those lacking resources

27 Affordable Housing Neighborhood

You are a consulting planner preparing a comprehensive plan for a city. The mayor, who has been in office for more than 30 years, has indicated that property owners of an older, in-town neighborhood want to rezone the property from single-family residential to office use. The city planner indicates the land-use plan should be changed for this neighborhood to reflect office use per the mayor. The mostly renter neighborhood is still stable but abuts the downtown commercial district, and for that reason has been identified in the plan already as a transitional neighborhood. Yet it is one of the few remaining in the city that provides affordable housing for low-income persons. How do you respond? (Carolin, Gerhart-Fritz, and Weitz 2012)

Commentary

The ethical planning practitioner will recognize opportunities to advance social justice, and this situation appears to be one of them (1.f). In this scenario, the mayor's inclination to reclassify the neighborhood for offices is debatable but plausibly justifiable. Before agreeing to make the change requested by the mayor and consented to by the city planner, you should bring to the mayor's attention other needs of the city, such as affordable housing for low-income households. You should also note the policy implications of changing the neighborhood land use from residential to office in the comprehensive plan.

For Further Discussion

Is the mayor's stance the client's decision? And if so, how do you balance principles 2.a and 2.b? If you feel strongly that the public interest dictates preserving the neighborhood for affordable housing rather than encouraging its conversion to office uses, would it be ethical to confront the mayor and disagree with him, making it an issue?

Relevant AICP Code Provisions

Principles to Which We Aspire

1.f. Social justice—plan for disadvantaged
2.a. Exercise independent judgment
2.b. Accept client decision unless illegal . . .

28 Urging a Modification of Exclusionary Zoning

Suppose a planner who works for a high-income suburb recognizes that the community's land development regulations are exclusionary. This makes it quite difficult for poor people or minority group members to live there, even though job opportunities for them exist in the area. The planner, as part of her regular job activities, decides to organize support from local people she knows are in favor of opening up the community so that they will put pressure on the suburban government's officials to change the community's zoning policy. In acting this way, does this planner behave ethically or unethically? (Howe and Kaufman 1979)

Commentary

The planner is definitely exercising independent professional judgment (2.a). Organizing support appears to be consistent with her aspiration to urge the alteration of policies, institutions, and decisions that oppose the needs of disadvantaged groups (1.f). Whether it is acceptable in light of principle 2.b is another consideration. In advocating for the needs of the disadvantaged, did the planner violate principle 1.h by singling them out (even if in this case they are specifically mentioned in the AICP Code) and not treating every other group the same? In the end, this type of activity may be considered ethical by some planners and unethical by others.

Relevant AICP Code Provisions

Principles to Which We Aspire

1.f. Social justice—plan for disadvantaged

1.h. Deal fairly and evenhandedly

2.a. Exercise independent judgment

2.b. Accept client decision unless illegal . . .

29 Preparing Estimates of Transit Ridership and Revenue

A city planner, who favors a low fare to make a proposed regional transit system more accessible to the poor, purposely develops estimates showing that the system will have high ridership and high revenue yield to counteract low ridership and low revenue yield estimates of regional planners who oppose a lower fare. Is this tactic ethical? (Howe and Kaufman 1979)

Commentary

The scenario leaves open the question of whether the planner's estimates are plausible, but his motivation is clear. That motivation could be justified, in part, by principles 1.e, 1.f, and 3.j, because the planner is looking out for the needs of transit-dependent populations and is contributing to groups that historically have lacked adequate planning resources and formal influence.

Despite these principles, my opinion is that the planner's action was not ethical, under the assumption that the estimates he came up with were not defensible and were crafted merely to counteract a policy decision he did not favor, which means he violated rule of conduct 1. However, if his estimates were defensible, preparing them could be considered ethical by some planners in light of the aspirational principles of the AICP Code. It would probably be difficult to allege the planner violated an enforceable rule of conduct, because projections cannot be verified as accurate or rejected as false. If rule 1 is taken out of play, it is up to the individual planner to make the call in this type of situation.

Relevant AICP Code Provisions

Principles to Which We Aspire

1.e. Participation—meaningful impact

1.f. Social justice—plan for disadvantaged

3.j. Contribute to those lacking resources

Rules of Conduct

1. Inaccurate information— untruthfulness

30 Planner Chooses Between Planning Firm and Minority Student Intern

You are a planning director in a city, and you are trying to get a housing conditions inventory finished over the summer so that the housing element of the city's comprehensive plan can be completed in time for review during the fall. You are considering, and have authority to approve, that the job be given to a local planning consulting firm; you have confidence that the firm can get the work done on a timely basis. Before you commit to that vendor, however, a minority undergraduate planning student shows up in your office and asks if there is any possibility of completing a summer internship with the city planning agency. The student submits her resume, which does not reveal any professional experience. Are there any ethical implications to your decision of whether to have the local planning consulting firm or the intern complete the housing conditions inventory?

Commentary

You have no obligation to the student intern. If you decide to hire the local planning consulting firm, that would be a reasoned decision. However, the AICP Code gives one reason (3.f) why you should seriously consider hiring the intern, if you are confident the work can be completed by the intern with competency and on time (2, preamble), under your staff's supervision.

Relevant AICP Code Provisions

Principles to Which We Aspire

2. (preamble) Competent performance
3.f. Contribute to professional development

Authority Director Evaluates Proposals

As the director of a municipal water and sewer authority, you are considering five proposals for work to prepare a mid-range utility extension plan for the city. A committee reviews the proposals and finds that all five firms have submitted responsive proposals and all five teams are qualified. The reviewers are required by the authority to apply a point-scoring scheme, and once the scores are tabulated, only a few points separate the highest-ranked and lowest-ranked proposals. There is no requirement in the authority's procurement rules to employ minorities, women, or disadvantaged groups. Only one of the firms proposes that minority contractors will work on the project. Are you under any ethical obligation to hire the firm with minority contractors?

Commentary

If the locality has not adopted an affirmative action policy, you are under no obligation to hire the firm with minority contractors. However, a decision to hire the firm that includes minority contractors would be one way to implement principle 3.g of the AICP Code.

Relevant AICP Code Provisions

Principles to Which We Aspire

3.g. Increase opportunity for under represented groups

32 Director Admonishes Planner for Excessive Volunteer Work

You are a county planner and an AICP member. You have signed out for several hours each week for the past six weeks to meet with a group of minority planning students at the university. You have been advising the minority students on their student projects, reviewing their resumes, conducting mock interviews, and advising them individually on how to pursue work leads upon graduation. The planning director of the county, concerned about your regular sign-outs, calls you into his office and admonishes you for being out of the office consistently to perform unrelated work for a number of hours during the work week over the past several weeks. He orders you to stop immediately. Are you justified in your effort to help university students on city time? Or is the planning director correct to order you to stop helping the university students?

Commentary

You are justified, and even encouraged, to undertake your activities with the minority students at the university, because they are consistent with two principles of the AICP Code (3.f and 3.g). However, the extent to which you are authorized to do so on your employer's time is another matter, as it takes away from your duties owed to your employer (2, preamble). You should defer to the planning director and cease doing the mentoring on your employer's time. You can always use personal time for these worthy endeavors or perhaps come to an agreement with the director to make up county government time you miss by mentoring the students.

Relevant AICP Code Provisions

Principles to Which We Aspire

2. (preamble) Competent performance

3.f. Contribute to professional development

3.g. Increase opportunity for underrepresented groups

33   Use of Technology in Citizen Participation

You are a senior planner in a city and are charged with crafting a community participation program for an update to the city's comprehensive plan. You recently attended a conference that had a session on using social media as a public participation technique. Excited about what you've learned, you decide on a three-pronged approach as the centerpiece of your participation strategy: First, the city's Facebook page will be the central mechanism for communication regarding the city's update of the comprehensive plan. Second, you plan to release a series of email blasts to notify residents and interested individuals about public workshops and to provide notice of material available for review. And third, you propose to employ a commercially available phone app to gain instant feedback from citizens about planning proposals. What ethical issues, if any, arise from the public participation strategy you have selected?

Commentary

At issue generally is the extent to which the chosen strategy will reach the intended range of planning participants. Computer and Internet use varies significantly by race and ethnicity; the lowest Internet usage rates in the United States are by black and Hispanic households (File 2013). Internet use differs by age group as well, with the lowest usage rates among people ages 55 and older and the highest rates for persons 35 years old and younger. Household income is also an important variable; only about 50 percent of low- and moderate-income households in the United States had access to the Internet in 2011 (File 2013). With regard to people's use of smartphones in the United States, there is not much variation by race or ethnicity, but there is significant variation in age. Furthermore, lower-income households in the United States are far less likely to visit social networking sites or own smartphones (Edison Research and Arbitron 2012).

Because the proposed participation strategy would leave out significant segments of society who cannot or will not participate, it would not reach all people in the planning jurisdiction and would therefore be inconsistent with principle 1.d to provide information to all affected persons. The participation strategy would limit, rather than expand, opportunities for all persons, and it would appear to miss connecting with lower- income households when planners have a "special responsibility to plan for the needs of the disadvantaged" (1.f). A strategy for public participation relying predominantly on the Internet and social media could amount to social injustice (Salkin and Tappendorf 2011). Similarly, it could be considered unfair to emphasize participation by Internet users to the exclusion of nonusers, thus violating principle 1.h. Principle 3.b would not be served, because the strategy would be focused on educating only a part, rather than all, of the public.

Relevant AICP Code Provisions

Principles to Which We Aspire

1.d. Provide information to all affected

1.f. Social justice—plan for disadvantaged

1.h. Deal fairly and evenhandedly

3.b. Educate public on planning issues

To meet these principles, the primarily Internet-based participation strategy would need to be supplemented with other mechanisms to reach audiences who don't have computers, Internet access, and smartphones. Social networking and the Internet generally may help meet public participation goals of planning projects, but planners must understand the limitations with regard to audiences reached.

34

Regional Agency Engaged in Multiple Planning Functions for County

A council of government (COG), including a planning division and an economic development division, is simultaneously preparing separate work products for the same rural county. The economic development division is preparing a grant application to extend sanitary sewer along a U.S. highway, past prime farmland, approximately three miles out of a city, to a small industrial park currently served by on-site septic systems. The planning division has drafted a land-use plan and zoning ordinance showing property along the highway corridor through which the sewer would be extended as agricultural land. Is there an ethical problem with this scenario?

Commentary

Although there is no enforceable misconduct, this scenario highlights a potentially embarrassing and serious failure on the COG's part to coordinate its own activities for the same client. Both the economic development and planning divisions should pay attention to the interrelatedness (1.c) and long-term consequences (1.b) of decision making for economic development and land-use planning. It could be considered incompetent (2, preamble) not to do so, thus being inconsistent with principles of the AICP Code. Further, once the economic development application is filed and the land-use plan is drafted, it will be difficult to reconcile them in any meaningful way.

Relevant AICP Code Provisions

Principles to Which We Aspire

1.b. Concern for long-range consequences

1.c. Attend to interrelatedness of decisions

2. (preamble) Competent performance

35 Planner Posts Statement on Social Media

You are a planner employed by a metropolitan planning organization (MPO). A new four-lane, divided highway on the fringe of the region has just been formally added by the MPO to its transportation improvement program, to be designed and constructed in future years. The local newspaper recently published a story about the MPO's decision to pursue the highway project. The people interviewed in the story debated the merits and liabilities of the project. The public became more interested in the project, and the debate and decision on the highway project prompted you to post a comment about the highway on your Facebook (or other social media) page. Your posted comment read literally as follows: "If constructed, the highway project will eventually lead to suburban sprawl, contrary to the regional growth management plan." Are there ethical issues associated with posting this comment on social media?

Commentary

On the basis of several principles, posting a comment on social media appears at first glance to be justified. The planner's posted statement reflects concern for the long-range consequences of a decision (1.b) in that it attends to the long-range impacts of the highway. It also reflects concern about the interrelationships of transportation and land use (1.c). Further, highway projects can have impacts on the natural environment and historic resources; thus posting the comment might be rationalized on the basis of principle 1.g, which aspires to protect the natural environment and preserve heritage. The planner may also consider the statement to be justified simply because it is educating the public about a planning issue (3.b) and sharing "the results of experience and research that contribute to the body of planning knowledge" (3.d).

Yet other principles are also relevant. Consider principle 1.d, which reads in full: "We shall provide timely, adequate, clear, and accurate information on planning issues to all affected persons and to governmental decision makers." Now that the MPO has made a decision to include the highway project in its plan and improvement program, is this a "planning issue" any longer? That is open to interpretation. The MPO has made a decision to pursue the project, so one interpretation is that the planning process for the project (at least this phase of it) has ended. However, the highway project could still be considered an ongoing planning issue because there are subsequent issues to be settled, such as design options available to mitigate impacts.

Your posted comment includes part opinion (the highway will lead to sprawl) and part verifiable description (sprawl is contrary to the regional growth management plan). If there is a policy in the regional growth management plan that discourages suburban sprawl, the descriptive part of your comment is factually correct (accurate) and in that regard is consistent with principle

Relevant AICP Code Provisions

Principles to Which We Aspire

1.b. Concern for long-range consequences

1.c. Attend to interrelatedness of decisions

1.d. Provide information to all affected

1.g. Excellent design; preserve heritage

2.b. Accept client decision unless illegal . . .

3.b. Educate public on planning issues

3.d. Share experience and research

Relevant Rules of Conduct

19. Concealment of interest/ failure to disclose

1.d. On the other hand, if there is no such policy, or you've loosely interpreted a similar policy, you have violated principle 1.d. The principle also suggests an obligation on the part of the planner to provide "information," but is social media a proper way to reach all of the public, including decision makers? Further, is it timely and appropriate to provide this information after the decision has been made to include the project in the improvement program? I question both the communication mechanism chosen and the timeliness of the planner's information about this issue (and consider them both to be probably inappropriate despite the fact they are supported by other code principles).

Consider also principle 2.b, which reads: "We shall accept the decisions of our client or employer concerning the objectives and nature of the professional services we perform unless the course of action is illegal or plainly inconsistent with our primary obligation to the public interest." Arguably, principle 2.b may not apply, since the decision by the MPO is separate and distinct from your work at the MPO, even if you were charged with evaluating the growth management implications of MPO project decisions. The MPO made a decision to include the highway in the improvement plan. The planner's statement could be viewed as nonacceptance of the decision of the MPO, which is the employer. Does principle 2.b mean that you must accept the decision? Not necessarily, in my view. The MPO's decision is not illegal, but a planner (after weighing benefits of the highway once constructed, such as a reduction of traffic congestion) could conceivably view the decision as inconsistent with the public interest (defined in other adopted plans such as the growth management plan). One's own interpretation of the public interest might be enough motivation for a planner to speak out against the decision or register discontent.

Finally, consider whether rule of conduct 19 is applicable. It reads: "We shall not fail to disclose the interests of our client or employer when participating in the planning process. Nor shall we participate in an effort to conceal the true interests of our client or employer." It is the first sentence of the rule that is potentially relevant. In posting the comment on social media, the planner did not disclose the interest of the MPO as the employer. Is the planner obligated under rule 19 in this instance to disclose reasons why the MPO approved the project? And, as an employee of the MPO, is the planner obligated by rule 19 to disclose his or her employment relationship with the MPO? These are tough questions without a clear answer, but I would play it safe and recommend that the planner disclose that he or she is an employee of the MPO, and to at least provide the rationale for the MPO's decision even if the planner disagrees with it.

The bigger lesson, in my view, is that posting comments on social media ican be fraught with ethical dangers. If you elect to use social media, be careful about wording and consider the AICP Code before posting.

36 Disclosure of Potential Environmental Impacts

You are a private-sector planner employed by a large consulting firm specializing in environmental impact reviews. You are working on a complex, large-dollar environmental impact review for a hospital. One of your staff members writes that there are idle oil wells adjacent to the proposed hospital site. Your research indicates that these wells have not been permanently decommissioned to meet environmental standards for permanent closure, and you tell your boss about your findings. Your boss says, "They are idle; we don't need to say anything more than that they are there and are idle." What do you do? (Carolin, Gerhart-Fritz, and Weitz 2012)

Commentary

You may at first be confronted with a sense of duty not to violate the judgment of your boss and thus to accept her decision as your client (2.b). However, you may aspire to grant allegiance to the public interest (1, preamble), to avoid harm to the environment and to preserve the integrity and heritage of the natural and built environment (1.g). And you also aspire to exercise independent judgment (2.a).

It would be up to the AICP ethics officer in the specific case of a misconduct charge to decide the meaning of the term "adequate," but in my view, aspiration (1.d) and the duty (rule of conduct 1) to provide adequate and accurate information should be interpreted to include the term "complete" information. This is admittedly more than a strict constructionist interpretation on my part. Furthermore, I would be worried that the failure to include the information you found might be considered "reckless indifference" or "deliberate" within the meaning of rule 1. In my view, the information you found about the oil wells not being properly decommissioned according to prevailing law or rule should not be excluded.

Does rule of conduct 18 apply? It reads: "we shall not direct or coerce other professionals to make analyses or reach findings not supported by available evidence." I would say no, it does not apply, at least in the sense that you are not being directed to make an unsubstantiated statement. Rather, your boss's directive relates to omitting certain information you believe is important. Thus there doesn't appear to be a violation of rule 18, but I have much trouble reconciling the boss's suggestion with rule 1.

Relevant AICP Code Provisions

Principles to Which We Aspire

1. (preamble) Professional integrity
1.d. Provide information to all affected
1.g. Excellent design; preserve heritage
2.a. Exercise independent judgment
2.b. Accept client decision unless illegal . . .

Rules of Conduct

1. Inaccurate information – untruthfulness
18. Pressure: unsubstantiated findings

37 Information Shared With Neighborhood Group

A city planner assigned to work with a particular low-income neighborhood gives information, without authorization, to the head of the neighborhood organization on a study being prepared by another planning agency unit, which recommends substantial land clearance in this neighborhood. Is this activity ethical? (Howe and Kaufman 1979)

Commentary

Addressing the rules of conduct first, the planner did not engage in discussions with decision makers in a manner prohibited by rules, procedures, or custom. Therefore, rule of conduct 9 doesn't apply directly. However, the planner engaged in private discussions with a low-income group, perhaps in a manner prohibited by the client in the sense that authorization was not gained in advance. Rule 1 would seem to require that the information be provided, because it involved a planning issue, but to whom was the planner obliged to give the information? Rule 9 is not clear in that regard. Principle 2.b presents a sticky ethical situation: Because the client did not specifically authorize the release of the information, the planner should not have released it unless he was driven by an overriding public interest, defined in such a way to include the various applicable principles of the AICP Code. Absent a clear rule of conduct to the contrary, the planner's action in this scenario is plausibly justifiable. However, shouldn't the information, if disclosed, be given to all relevant client groups—even those opposing the planner's views—per principle 1.h?

Relevant AICP Code Provisions

Principles to Which We Aspire

1.h. Deal fairly and evenhandedly
2.b. Accept client decision unless illegal . . .

Rules of Conduct

1. Inaccurate information—untruthfulness
9. Private communication (other)

38 Planning Director Excludes Junior Planners' Observations

You are a county planning director, and your agency is required by law to conduct a review of public agency plans and major development proposals. You receive an application from the city airport authority to review an airport master plan update. You view this application as routine, because you know the runway expansion called for in the plan update is much needed for enhancing local economic development prospects. The expansion will go ahead, you reason, because federal funding is already secured, pending plan adoption and Federal Aviation Administration final approval. You assign the review to two junior planners. One notes that, in order to protect the approach zone of the proposed extended runway, the plan update calls for the purchase of land in an adjacent developed, historic, low-income minority neighborhood; the planner recommends that the impacts on the neighborhood be assessed in your agency's report and mitigated. The other planner notes that the drainage plan directs the expanded runway's surface water runoff onto an abutting cemetery; that planner recommends that drainage be discussed in the agency report and mitigated. You read the memos from the junior planners but ultimately elect to include neither of the planners' observations and suggestions in your agency report. Your reasoning is that you consider plan approval a done deal, because of the airport expansion's advantages for economic development and the prearranged funding; further, addressing the matters raised by the junior planners may cause delay in airport expansion and possibly even the loss of funding. Is it unethical to exclude the junior planners' observations and suggestions?

Commentary

Excluding the junior planners' observations and suggestions is unethical in my view. The points raised by the junior planners are "planning issues" and should be brought to the attention of decision makers (1.d), regardless of the prospect that to do so could result in expensive mitigation for the client. To withhold certain information from the report means that the other information provided therein is inadequate, in my view. An ethical planning practitioner will pay special attention to the impacts of the airport plan on the low-income neighborhood, which is probably disadvantaged (1.f). Although perhaps outside the context and intent, principle 3.d seems to suggest that you should share the findings of the junior planners. To withhold the information offered by them would seem to violate rule of conduct 1. Similarly, by deliberately excluding the findings of the junior planners, you have arguably violated rule 10, because exclusion of information could mean that the information has been misrepresented.

Relevant AICP Code Provisions

Principles to Which We Aspire

1.d. Provide information to all affected

1.f. Social justice—plan for disadvantaged

3.d. Share experience and research

Rules of Conduct

1. Inaccurate information—untruthfulness

10. Misrepresentation of others' qualifications

39 Reporter Requests All Information on Pending Development Project

You are a mid-level planner and an AICP member. You are assigned to write a rezoning recommendation on a project. Notice of the application has been published in the newspaper, but the staff report has not been written or released. You have been collecting information and have various notes and the beginnings of a draft report in the file. A local newspaper reporter has called the director and asked for the agency file on the development project, including all applicable materials produced to date by the local planning agency. The director, who is also an AICP member, directs you to give the information (data you have collected) to the newspaper reporter but to exclude any draft report on the application. The director explains that this particular newspaper reporter previously published an article about a development project that distorted information and stirred up controversy in advance of the rezoning decision. What information do you give to the reporter? (Based on Howe 1994)

Commentary

Although he did mention something about this reporter stirring up trouble, the primary motivation on the part of the director seems to be to avoid releasing partial work that is in draft form and has not been subjected to review. It is not prudent to release a draft of a planning report until it has been through the entire staff review process, including the director's review and approval. You should follow the directive of the planning director. Though rule of conduct 1 applies to this scenario, it does not necessarily obligate you or the director to release a draft report not yet ready for public consumption. However, giving objective information already collected is appropriate, considering rule 1 and the director's authorization to release information.

Relevant AICP Code Provisions

Rules of Conduct

1. Inaccurate information— untruthfulness

40 Utility Company Maintenance Facility

You are the town planner for a small, historic town. Design controls adopted by the town are limited to building and landscaping review by the town planner before the issuing of a permit. A utility company has applied to establish a maintenance facility on a site in town along the main highway. The company is accustomed to having its way and sometimes will claim that it does not have to follow local site plan requirements, zoning rules, and design guidelines. The site plan shows the vehicle bays, which have roll-up overhead doors, facing the state highway. Also, it proposes a chain-link fence topped with barbed wire paralleling the state highway frontage. Areas are designated on the site plan for outdoor storage in the front yard, and only two small-caliber trees are shown on the planting plan along the property's highway frontage. You think the project could look a lot better, but the town's controls are limited. As the town planner, how do you proceed with the site plan application?

Commentary

Because of inadequate local requirements addressing aesthetics, you may be tempted to bluff your way with the utility company if you want enhancement to the aesthetics of the utility installation site. The only other alternative, it seems, is to request that the utility company voluntarily comply with your desire to improve the design of the site. You are supposed to exercise independent judgment (2.a) and promote excellence of design (1.g). But do these principles outweigh other principles requiring you to treat the applicant fairly and to shoot straight with the applicant regarding what is required and what isn't (1.d and 1.h)? Of course, if you bluff, even for a good purpose, you lose integrity, and the utility company representatives can easily read the town's code and discover you are bluffing. In my view, bluffing may rise to the level of a violation of rule of conduct 1. You can request improvements but should not engage in trying to bluff the utility company into thinking that your demands for better aesthetics are actual code requirements.

Relevant AICP Code Provisions

Principles to Which We Aspire

1.d. Provide information to all affected

1.g. Excellent design; preserve heritage

1.h. Deal fairly and evenhandedly

2.a. Exercise independent judgment

Rules of Conduct

1. Inaccurate information—untruthfulness

41 Service on Consultant Proposal Review Committee

You are a county planner serving as part of a committee charged with reviewing and recommending the best consultant proposal. The county's contracts manager has come up with a quantitative scoring scheme to rate each proposal. Your boss, the county planning director, has a favorite consulting firm and instructs you to fudge your original numbers so that the consulting firm the director wants will score the highest. What should you do? (Based on APA 2012)

Commentary

There are rules of conduct that make participation in this type of activity unethical. Because they are written with a limited context, some of the rules of conduct cited here do not apply to this scenario, but they are cited because, taken together, they clearly identify this behavior as unethical and steer us away from it. Though I see direct violations (explained below), I also tend to argue for a full reading of the AICP Code and an extension of the rules of conduct beyond their strictly construed circumstances.

There are many reasons pertaining to the rules of conduct that make it unethical for you to follow the instructions of the county planning director. If you do so, you will fail to provide accurate information. Though this is admittedly not a "planning issue," such a failure is contrary to rule of conduct 1. To the extent the city's personnel regulations or procurement rules make favoritism unlawful, you will violate rule 2. The most direct violation of the AICP Code is probably rule 10; if you agree to fudge the scoring scheme, you will deliberately misrepresent your authentic, original findings regarding other professionals who are more qualified in your own assessment. By doing so, you will also fail to exercise independent professional judgment (2.a). Though rule of conduct 12 is limited to planners' own qualifications, if you acquiesce to your boss, you will be agreeing to misstate the qualifications of other professionals, in violation of the spirit—if not the very limited context—of that rule. Similarly, although you would not be selling your own services in such a way that rule 13 applies, your action would clearly amount to participation in an effort to influence decisions by improper means, violating the spirit of that rule of conduct. If you participate in the fudging of scores, you will violate rule of conduct 19, because you would be participating in an effort to conceal the true interests of your client or employer, which is clearly favoritism and thus not based on an objective review of the proposals.

Relevant AICP Code Provisions

Principles to Which We Aspire
2.a. Exercise independent judgment

Rules of Conduct
1. Inaccurate information—untruthfulness
2. Illegal or unethical conduct
10. Misrepresentation of others' qualifications
12. Misstatement of one's qualifications
13. Influence via improper means
18. Pressure: unsubstantiated findings
19. Concealment of interest/failure to disclose
25. Deliberate, wrongful act

Your boss, if an AICP member, has clearly violated rule of conduct 18 in directly coercing another person on the proposal evaluation committee to "reach findings not supported by available evidence." If you acquiesce to your boss's request, both you and your boss could be subject to charges that you undertook a deliberately wrongful act, in violation of rule 25.

42 Planner Asked to Recommend Professionals

You are a mid-level planner in a city, and you are charged with advising development applicants on what is needed to comply with the zoning ordinance and city development regulations. Applicants often need a land survey, variance application, floodplain permit, plot plan, or other document. In such cases, development applicants who are not local frequently ask if you can recommend good private companies they can use to complete the necessary surveys, plans, permit applications, or other work. Having been confronted with this question before, the agency prepared a list of land surveying, landscape architecture, engineering, and land planning companies that have completed work with the city in the past. You provide that list to the inquiring development applicants. Are there ethical issues with your action? (Based on APA 2012)

Commentary
Providing the list of professional firms to the development applicant seems appropriate and is probably done by a number of planning agencies, though there is some risk associated with doing so. Commenting on specific firms, or answering questions about the success and effectiveness of the professional firms on the list, is not advised (see also APA 2012). Another suggestion is that you offer to let applicants look at prior work submitted by firms, so they can get some sense of the quality of work for themselves.

For Further Discussion
What if, in addition to providing the list, you also suggest that one of the companies on the list is particularly effective and successful in doing business with the city? Or, to the contrary, what if you tell development applicants that there are a couple of firms on the list that you view as not very competent? Your biases could lead to misrepresentation of others' qualifications, potentially in violation of rule of conduct 10.

Relevant AICP Code Provisions

Principles to Which We Aspire

1.a. Consider rights of others

Rules of Conduct

10. Misrepresentation of others' qualifications

43 Use of One Firm's Product by Another Firm

Two planning consulting firms (A and B) routinely form a team and have worked on several projects together. Firm A, in interviewing on its own for contract work with a prospective client, delivers a PowerPoint presentation that includes descriptions of planning projects that both firms worked on jointly. In the presentation, the graphics used by Firm A in one of the descriptions were prepared by Firm B but not specifically credited to Firm B. Does this action violate the AICP Code?

Commentary

By using in its presentation the graphics of another firm that is not part of their proposed team, Firm A violates rule of conduct 17. Firm A also violates rule 11, because this conduct occurs in the process of soliciting work and involves the release of misleading information. Similarly, Rule of Conduct 12 applies, because by including the graphics of another firm without specifically citing the source, Firm A is implicitly—though possibly inadvertently—claiming that the graphics are Firm A's work, which is a misstatement of professional qualifications. Planning Firm A used the graphics without permission and thus was not being conscious of the rights of the firm that owns the work. This is not treatment that is fair (3.c) or that considers the rights of others (1.a).

For Further Discussion

Does it make a difference if Firm B gives Firm A permission to use the graphics?

Relevant AICP Code Provisions

Principles to Which We Aspire

1.a. Consider rights of others
3.c. Treat other professionals fairly

Rules of Conduct

11. Solicitation via false claims; duress
12. Misstatement of one's qualifications
17. Misuse of others' work

44 Planner Prevented from Speaking Publicly in Opposition to Transportation Plan

A metropolitan planning organization (MPO) has prepared an update to the region's long-range transportation plan. A junior planner in a municipality within the region served by the MPO is opposed to the MPO's plan and has expressed opposition to his supervisor, the city planning director. But the city planning director supports the plan update. The junior planner expresses his intent to speak publicly in opposition to the plan update at the next public hearing held by the MPO. The city planning director refuses to allow the junior planner to express public opposition to the plan, and the director threatens to fire the junior planner if he disobeys her order not to speak publicly in opposition to the plan update. What should the junior planner do? (Based on Finkler 1971)

Commentary

The junior planner should prepare to speak and should lodge a complaint with the city planning director's supervisor. The junior planner should have the right to speak his mind as a private individual on any public policy matter. The city planning director does not have authority to disallow him to speak out on an issue. The director has ignored the rights of the junior planner (1.a), treated him unfairly (1.h), and denied him the opportunity to have a meaningful impact on a plan (1.e). If the junior planner wants to speak publicly on the plan at the hearing before the MPO, he could do so under the auspices that he wants to educate the public about planning issues and their relevance to everyday lives (3.b). The planning director has not commented on the views of the junior planner in a fair and professional manner (3.c) and instead has directed that those views be censored.

While rule of conduct 18 doesn't match this scenario perfectly, the planning director is clearly directing the junior planner not to publicly share his views. The director is, in essence, substituting her judgment for the junior planner's findings and conclusions. Because the junior planner would presumably have some evidence to support his views, her action potentially violates rule 18.

Rather than censure the junior planner for his contrasting views, the planning director should aspire to contribute time to the professional development of young professionals (3.f). Maybe the director can get the young professional to better understand why she supports the MPO's plan and why the junior planner should see the error in his views. Consistent with rule 19, if the junior planner wants to speak in opposition at the hearing, he can, but he should disclose that he is an employee of the city and that the official position of the city is different from his, as expressed by the planning director.

The planning director may believe that the junior planner owes loyalty to the department and to her, as senior spokes-

Relevant AICP Code Provisions

Principles to Which We Aspire

1.a. Consider rights of others
1.e. Participation—meaningful impact
1.h. Deal fairly and evenhandedly
2.b. Accept client decision unless illegal . . .
3.b. Educate public on planning issues
3.c. Treat other professionals fairly
3.f. Contribute to professional development

Rules of Conduct

18. Pressure: unsubstantiated findings
19. Concealment of interest/ failure to disclose

person in the city for planning matters. But principle 2.b does not apply in this scenario, because the junior planner, if he speaks at the MPO public hearing, is acting as a private citizen, not an employee of the city (so long as he makes that point clear). It seems unlikely that the city's personnel rules would support the planning director in her quest to fire the junior planner.

45 Private Correspondence on Local Government Email System

You are a private consultant working under contract to prepare design guidelines for a corridor in a local government jurisdiction. You have a planner on your consulting team who is employed full time by a different local government. The moonlighting planner frequently corresponds with you about the consulting project using the email address and computer system of the local government that employs her full time. What should you do?

Commentary

You should suggest to the planner that her actions constitute misconduct. Because the planner is using her public employer's email system toward a private end unrelated to the primary performance of her duties, she is not being diligent in performing her client's work (2, preamble), especially if she has corresponded with you on her employer's time. Even if the planner crafted the correspondence on her own time, however, she should not use the public email system. The planner has allowed a conflict to surface between her primary duties to her primary employer and the secondary concerns of her consulting client. That conflict is inconsistent with principle 2.c of the AICP Code.

It is apparent that the planner has also violated rules of conduct. It is reasonable to assume that the public agency employing the planner has rules regarding use of the public email system for private reasons. The planner should not have accepted an assignment with the consulting firm if it meant engaging in conduct contrary to the personnel regulations of her employer. Thus, she may be in violation of rule of conduct 2. If she accepted the assignment without disclosing it to, and seeking the permission of, her primary employer, then the planner has violated rule 4. The planner has used her public office—or, more precisely, the equipment associated with it— for a private reason, which is to gain the advantage of additional income. Because that private gain is not in the public interest of her primary employer, the planner has violated rule of conduct 14. Similarly, rule 25 is violated to the extent the planner is found to have acted with reckless indifference and committed a wrongful act that reflects poorly on the fitness of the planning profession.

Relevant AICP Code Provisions

Principles to Which We Aspire

2. (preamble) Competent performance
2.c. Avoid appearance of conflict of interest

Rules of Conduct

2. Illegal or unethical conduct
4. Outside employment ("moonlighting")
14. Official power used for advantage
25. Deliberate, wrongful act

46 City Manager Urges Change of Planning Staff Recommendation

An application for a conditional use permit has been filed in the city planning department where you work. You have prepared a staff report recommending denial on the basis of objective standards in the zoning ordinance. Prior to publishing the report, the city manager urges you to change the recommendation to approval, because the applicant is a friend of the mayor. How do you respond to the city manager?

Commentary

Providing a recommendation not in accord with the zoning ordinance, against your independent professional recommendation and inconsistent with the AICP Code, would violate rule of conduct 2. You should carefully explain to the city manager your ethical obligations under the AICP Code, which do not permit you to base your recommendation on his suggested criterion of favoritism. Then you should firmly reject the urgings of the city manager.

Rule of conduct 14 does not allow for the use of power, including administrative discretion, to obtain a special advantage, whether that advantage accrues to one's self (as implied in the rule of conduct) or to any other person, such as the mayor's friend. Changing the zoning recommendation could be considered a deliberately wrongful act, violating rule 25.

You will violate rule of conduct 18 if you respond to the pressure of the city manager by directing or coercing another planner on staff to reach findings favorable to the mayor's friend but not supported by the evidence.

Because there are multiple apparent violations of enforceable rules of conduct, it is not necessary to discuss in detail the inconsistencies with the aspirational principles of Section A of the AICP Code that would arise if you followed the city manager's urgings (1 preamble; 1.d, 1.h, 2.a, 2.c, 3.a). However, one principle is worth noting here. Principle 2.b could be read as a duty to accept the decisions of our client or employer—but not in this case, because the course of action would be, if not illegal, plainly inconsistent with our primary obligation to the public interest and the AICP Code.

For Further Discussion

What if, after you have rejected the request, the city manager indicates that he requires a planning staff recommendation and it must be a favorable one, regardless of your professional ethics? And what if the city manager adds, "If you don't write it, you will be fired"?

Relevant AICP Code Provisions

Principles to Which We Aspire

1. (preamble). Professional integrity
1.d. Provide information to all affected
1.h. Deal fairly and evenhandedly
2.a. Exercise independent judgment
2.b. Accept client decision unless illegal . . .
2.c. Avoid appearance of conflict of interest
3.a. Enhance professional integrity

Rules of Conduct

2. Illegal or unethical conduct
14. Official power used for advantage
18. Pressure: unsubstantiated findings
25. Deliberate, wrongful act

47
Preparing Grant Applications for Free in Anticipation of Project Award for Fee

Staff members at a public agency ask a private consulting firm to help prepare a grant application for free, with the implication that if the public agency is awarded the grant, the consulting firm will then get to work on the project for a fee. The public agency staff members make this request even though the grant requires a Request for Qualifications/Request for Proposal (RFQ/RFP) process to ensure open competition. The consulting firm agrees to the arrangement. Is this ethical? Would it make a difference if the private consulting firm was paid to write the grant application? (Carolin, Gerhart-Fritz, and Weitz 2012)

Commentary

In the consulting sector, the word used to describe the arrangement proposed by the public agency is "wired." Unfortunately, such arrangements may be more common than we would hope. The public agency has compromised the competitive process before it has even started. The agency has ignored the rights of other consultants to a fair process to compete for the work, in contradiction to principle 1.a. The agency's actions might even possibly rise to the level of discrimination, in violation of rule of conduct 20. Clearly, by describing tasks and writing them in the RFQ/RFP, the consulting firm can unfairly tailor the work scope in its own favor, which would not be ethical.

Procurement policies and rules of agencies are likely to address this situation in some indirect, if not direct, way, so they must be observed. If the consulting firm is selected for the project, rule 2 would make it unethical for the firm to accept a contract if agency rules were violated in the competitive bidding process. The consulting firm probably does not violate the strict language of rule 11, though the firm is clearly soliciting business by agreeing to write the RFQ/RFP. If the agency administrator is the one who has ultimate authority to decide which firm or team gets awarded the contract, all discussions between agency personnel and the consulting firm in preparing the RFQ/RFP could violate rule of conduct 8, though this scenario goes well beyond what most would normally consider a "planning process."

A key issue is whether the agency discloses that arrangement. Disclosure by the agency in the RFQ/RFP seems to me to be the only way to ensure fairness to other firms. If the agency discloses that one firm wrote the RFQ/RFP, however, other consultants will read that disclosure, consider the project wired, and probably not give serious consideration to bidding on it. The question of whether the consulting firm is paid to write the RFQ/RFP does not seem to matter, as the facts and conclusions about rules of conduct would not seem to change as a result.

Relevant AICP Code Provisions

Principles to Which We Aspire
1.a. Consider rights of others

Rules of Conduct
2. Illegal or unethical conduct
8. Private communication (public)
11. Solicitation via false claims; duress
20. Unlawful discrimination

48

Executive Director of Council of Government Has History of Suspect Practices

You are a planner working for a council of government (COG). During the past two years at the agency, you have lost respect for, and now distrust, the executive director of the council, because he has done some illegal or unethical things, such as employing suspect accounting practices, showing favoritism to certain contractors, and having an affair with someone in the agency. You have done nothing about your concerns to date. Now, after a change in board leadership at the COG, a personnel committee of the board governing the council has set up a process to evaluate the executive director. You have been asked to comment on his performance. What do you say to the COG officers on the personnel committee? (Based on Howe 1994)

Commentary

Some may contend that the principles cited, which refer to planning issues and processes (1.d, 1.h, 2.b, 3.c), could not reasonably be extended to a personnel matter. However, in my view, the principles and rules of the AICP Code should sometimes be read as if they extend beyond their strict context. Literally construing every rule and aspirational principle of the code without some liberal interpretation is likely to lead to an overly narrow view of professional ethics. For instance, rule of conduct 1 requires planners to provide adequate and timely information about planning issues, but this is a personnel matter.

Rule of conduct 2 indicates that "we shall not accept an assignment" under the circumstances here. But you have already accepted work for the agency, so rule 2 would not apply. However, in my view, the ethical planning practitioner would periodically, if not constantly, consider whether continuing an assignment is justified. The executive director has engaged in illegal conduct, and you now have an opportunity to blow the whistle on him. If the executive director is an AICP member, he appears to have engaged in misconduct according to the AICP Code. You must be careful not to misrepresent the actions of the executive director (10).

Relevant AICP Code Provisions

Principles to Which We Aspire

1.d. Provide information to all affected

1.h. Deal fairly and evenhandedly

2.b. Accept client decision unless illegal . . .

3.c. Treat other professionals fairly

Rules of Conduct

2. Illegal or unethical conduct

10. Misrepresentation of others' qualifications

Regional Planner Seeks Elected Position

You work as staff for a council of government and want to run for elected office in the city where you reside, which is located in the regional jurisdiction of the council. Does the pursuit of elected office raise ethical issues for you?

Commentary

Politically active planners—dubbed "closet politicians" by Howe (1994)—may be frustrated by the limits of their positions as planners and strive to make a bigger difference in shaping and even adopting public policies consistent with principles to which the planning profession aspires. Some might go so far as to argue that everyone, including planners, has a civic duty to participate in a democracy, such as through seeking elected positions if they believe they are equipped and capable. You would bring professional knowledge to the elected position, and the position would give you the opportunity to educate the public and move municipal policy toward many of the ends the planning profession advocates.

But before you run for elected office, you should consult your employer's personnel regulations to check whether such an action is condoned or otherwise addressed. Elected positions do come with some remuneration, so it could be considered outside employment, though not necessarily in planning or a related profession. To be safe, you should seek written approval to run for the elected position, in the spirit of rule of conduct 4, even if it could be reasonably argued that rule 4 does not apply.

Relevant AICP Code Provisions

Rules of Conduct

4. Outside employment ("moonlighting")

50 Part-Time Consultant and Full-Time City Planner Job

Your full-time position working as a planner for a city government was reduced to part time, because the economy was poor and there was a major reduction in development activity in the city. To supplement your reduced salary, you started a private consulting business. About a year later, the city brought you back to full-time status. Is it unethical for you to keep your consulting business while maintaining the full-time city planner position? (Carolin, Gerhart-Fritz, and Weitz 2012)

Commentary

You needed to acquire written permission from the city to engage in private consulting, per rule of conduct 4. If you did not, then you violated this rule.

Naturally, a planner who has established reliable clients in the consulting field and has good prospects for repeat business or continuing contracts might not want to lose momentum and give up the consulting business. A planner can quickly get accustomed to higher wages as a consultant compared with most public-sector planner salaries in city governments. Can a planner do both jobs well? If you work a full-time city planner job and moonlight by engaging in private consulting work, sooner or later your endurance will be compromised, and something will have to give. If and when a work deadline must be sacrificed, it would be natural for you to be more concerned with your consulting work. It would not be fair to the local government for you to take a full-time salary and not complete full-time work in exchange, with the diligence expected of you per the AICP Code.

In the long run, this dual role is likely to present problems, and additional ethical issues will probably manifest. It is best, from an ethical standpoint, for you to choose between either continuing to consult or working in the full-time position with the city, and not to attempt to pursue both simultaneously. If you are confident that your restored full-time employment with the local government is relatively safe and permanent, with local government permission, you could continue to moonlight until you complete existing consulting contracts and agreements.

For those searching for a middle ground, you could ask to decline the additional public-sector hours and keep the consultancy, presuming you have the permission of your local government employer, per rule of conduct 4. Such a request may not be granted, because the local government may want you to work full-time or not at all. If you are successful in gaining local government approval to maintain your status quo arrangement combining part-time consulting and your part-time public sector position, the same type of ethical conflicts might arise as with working full-time for the city and moonlighting as a consultant.

Relevant AICP Code Provision

Rules of Conduct

4. Outside employment ("moonlighting")

51

Planning Director Opposes and Testifies in Court Against Rezoning Decision

An application is made by a property owner to rezone several hundred acres of waterfront property from low-density residential to heavy industrial. The county's land-use plan recommends residential use at varying densities. With his staff's input, the county's planning director writes a recommendation for denial, based on the proposed rezoning's inconsistency with the county's land-use plan, environmental concerns, and potential detriment to scenic features of the waterfront site. The county planning commission recommends the heavy industrial zoning for the property, and the county board of commissioners approves it. Residents of a neighborhood near the property file suit in court against the rezoning. The planning director provides some behind-the-scenes assistance to the neighborhood group as it prepares its case, and he testifies in court against the rezoning. Do the planning director's assistance to the neighborhood group and testimony constitute a conflict of interest, or are they otherwise unethical? (Based on Finkler 1971)

Commentary

In this scenario, the planning director has entirely discarded any of the interests of his employer, the county, in favor of his own conception of the public interest. He engaged in a direct conflict of interest (2.c) by accepting an assignment to appear in court and testify against the merit of his employer's decision.

Once the board of commissioners made the policy decision to deny the rezoning, the planning director had the duty not to undermine his employer's decision, which is final, subject to litigation. Yet he worked to undermine the county's decision by testifying against his employer—and in doing so, engaged in additional misconduct, as described below.

It is tempting to begin by questioning the motives of the planning director for taking these actions. Either he no longer cares about his county job, or he must have felt very strongly that the industrial development would have a major, detrimental impact on the community ecosystem. The planning director could at least argue, in defense, that his conception of the public interest trumps all other considerations of the code, including his obligation to accept his employer's decisions (2.b). But an aspirational principle cannot trump the rules of conduct, because it is the rules of conduct, not the principles, which are enforceable.

In this case, probably the most solid support for the conclusion that the planning director committed misconduct under the AICP Code is rule 4. Let us assume that testimony in court is "employment" and related to the planning profession. Let us also assume that the planner did not gain his employer's express written permission to testify in court against the employer's rezoning decision—after all, why would the county give such permission? If these assumptions are correct, the planning director has violated rule of conduct 4. His actions

Relevant AICP Code Provisions

Principles to Which We Aspire

2.b. Accept client decision unless illegal . . .

2.c. Avoid appearance of conflict of interest

Rules of Conduct

4. Outside employment ("moonlighting")
5. Acceptance of gifts or advantage
7. Breach of confidentiality
14. Official power used for advantage
19. Concealment of interest/ failure to disclose
25. Deliberate, wrongful act

might also be considered a deliberately wrongful act, thus a violation of rule of conduct 25.

The planning director could also have a problem with rule of conduct 5 if he was paid by the neighborhood group to appear in court, as his court appearance came about, by and large, because of his role as a county employee. If he was paid to appear in court, perhaps the planning director is also vulnerable to a charge that his court appearance resulted from his use of the power of his county position and that he gained special advantage that is not in the public interest (14).

There are equally plausible conditions under which the planning director has also violated rule of conduct 7. As a county employee participating in the process of rezoning, he may be privy to confidential information about the case. Local government attorneys typically direct the county's official zoning file (when the subject of litigation) to be held in its custody for confidentiality purposes. To the extent the planning director revealed any confidential information in the litigation process, he may have violated rule 7.

If one accepts the argument that subsequent litigation is part of the "planning process," then the planning director had the duty at least to disclose the interests of his client or employer (rule 19). Further, I would argue—perhaps outside the realm of the AICP Code's language—that the planning director had a duty not only to disclose the county's interest but, even more important, to defend the county's position even if he disagreed with it, so long as the rezoning decision remained an issue and so long as he was a county employee.

Property to Be Rezoned Touches Property Owned by Family Member

You are a junior-level county planner who prepares staff reports on rezoning matters; reports are finalized by the senior planner in consultation with the planning director. You are almost finished with a staff report on a rezoning application, and the initial recommendation is for approval because the requested rezoning category is consistent with the land-use plan recommendation for low-density residential use. In preparing graphics for the report, however, you discover that a point of the subject property touches a point of property owned by one of your family members. What should you do?

Commentary

Ownership of property by a family member could compromise the independent professional judgment you aspire to exercise (2.a). This situation could be easily perceived as a conflict of interest, if it is not a direct conflict (2.c).

Does rule of conduct 6 apply? You are performing work on a project for your employer, and an affirmative recommendation on the residential rezoning of property touching your family member's property could influence the local governing body's decision to approve the rezoning. There is the possibility that the residential zoning could result in gain to your family member—albeit in much more of an indirect than direct manner, because it cannot be proven that a rezoning decision on one property directly increases property values on abutting land.

Although the connection between the rezoning recommendation and a potential increase in property values on abutting property is not direct, you should write a memo to your supervisors disclosing the interest, discuss it with them, and let them decide if it is appropriate to uphold the staff recommendation as you penned it, or if it should be rewritten. If you do not make such a disclosure, there could be a perception that you are using the public office of planner toward a private advantage. That would be improper and might violate rule of conduct 14.

If you have the private interests of your family member in mind and recommend approval based on the possibility of private benefit (that is, increased property value) accruing to a family member, rather than on adopted standards for land-use plan map changes, you might also violate rule 18, because it could be construed that you are coercing supervisors to reach an opinion not based on proper criteria. Failure to disclose would be inconsistent with the AICP Code in that it would be deliberately wrong, for the reasons described above, and would not reflect positively on the planning profession's fitness (rule 25).

Relevant AICP Code Provisions

Principles to Which We Aspire

2.a. Exercise independent judgment
2.c. Avoid appearance of conflict of interest

Rules of Conduct

6. Personal or financial gain
14. Official power used for advantage
18. Pressure: unsubstantiated findings
25. Deliberate, wrongful act

53 Information Leaked Regarding Plans for Parking Deck Downtown

You are an AICP member and the director of a downtown development authority in a medium-sized town. Members of the authority's board have for some time wanted to increase parking availability in the downtown, and the downtown plan calls for addressing future parking needs but is not specific as to how that goal will be accomplished. You are aware that the downtown abuts a low-income minority neighborhood that is opposed to expansion of the downtown. The authority's board met in closed session to consider purchasing real estate at the edge of downtown and the minority neighborhood. The information is confidential because it involves real estate matters, and the board, by law, is specifically authorized to meet in closed sessions to discuss real estate. You were at the meeting, at which you learned that the board wants to purchase an available site and construct a four-story parking deck. You shared knowledge of the board's intent with a close friend, who is a minority. In turn, your friend leaked to the press the authority's intent to purchase the property and construct the parking deck. What are the ethical implications, and what do you now do as downtown development authority director?

Commentary

The chief issue in this scenario is whether you erred in releasing, intentionally or not, the information about the board's intent to acquire real estate. Different rules of conduct would lead you in opposite directions, and the principles in Section A of the code (listed in the box at right) would tend to support a notion of the public interest that is amenable to the release of the information, perhaps even in spite of its confidentiality.

One must examine the lengthy rule of conduct 7 closely. Your disclosure of confidential information was not required by law, and it was not required to prevent a clear violation of law. Further, the information, while important, was not required to be released to prevent a substantial injury to the public. It appears you have violated rule 7.

But let's examine other relevant rules. Rule of conduct 1 requires you "to provide adequate, timely, clear and accurate information on planning issues." Isn't the board's intent to purchase the property in order to construct the parking deck a planning issue? Could it be argued that there was no public interest in keeping the matter confidential, or was the breach of confidentiality contradictory to the development authority's interest, in that it risked inflating the expectations of the owner of the site proposed for acquisition?

And what about rule of conduct 19? It provides that "we shall not fail to disclose the interests of our client or employer when participating in the planning process." When does the planning process start? Rule 19 also provides: "Nor shall we participate in an effort to conceal the true interests of our client or employer." Would keeping the information confidential be concealment of interests? What relative weight should the vari-

Relevant AICP Code Provisions

Principles to Which We Aspire

1.d. Provide information to all affected

1.e. Participation – meaningful impact

1.f. Social justice – plan for disadvantaged

1.g. Excellent design; preserve heritage

1.h. Deal fairly and evenhandedly

2.a. Exercise independent judgment

Rules of Conduct

1. Inaccurate information – untruthfulness

7. Breach of confidentiality

19. Concealment of interest/ failure to disclose

ous aspirational principles have when put in the mix of a conflict between two or more rules of conduct? Don't the principles in Section A of the code demonstrate a need (if not an obligation) to be proactive in the interest of the needs and desires of the disadvantaged, who don't presumably have power and a voice in the process?

By not sharing the information with your close friend, you could have prevented a potentially serious allegation of misconduct for violating confidentiality. Having not intended to release the information does not absolve you of your failure to maintain confidentiality. Without the leak, the information would have been funneled out through the proper channels. You are required to meet the rules of the AICP Code, yet you jumped the gun and violated confidentiality. Due to the specificity of the process outlined in rule of conduct 7, you would probably be found guilty of violating it. In your defense, you would also have multiple code citations, both aspirational principles and rules, to cite in support of the release of information at the time it was released.

Structure With Historical Value About to Be Demolished

As a historic preservation planning consultant, you conducted a multiproperty survey of a neighborhood and produced a documentation report for a client. That survey and report showed that one of the properties has unique historical value not otherwise recognized in public documents. You signed a confidentiality agreement with the client promising not to share any of the survey or report results with another person, firm, or agency. You are concerned when you read in the paper that the city urban redevelopment agency is scheduled to purchase and demolish a block of buildings, including the property that has unique historical value. What do you do?

Commentary

You signed a confidentiality agreement, and you will therefore violate rule of conduct 7 if you disclose the historical value of the property. In light of principles 1.d, 1.g, and 3.d, and rule of conduct 1, you could seek a modification of the confidentiality agreement that would allow you to disclose the historical value of the property. However, if the client is unavailable or refuses to allow disclosure of the report's finding, you should not disclose the information that you are required to hold inviolate. There is enough support in the AICP Code, however, to make an opposite conclusion: Some planners in this instance might believe that their conscientiously attained notion of the public interest (to protect historical resources) would override obligations of confidentiality to a past client. I disagree, given the specificity of the language in rule 7. An enforceable rule would trump the aspirational principle.

Relevant AICP Code Provisions

Principles to Which We Aspire
1.a. Consider rights of others
1.d. Provide information to all affected
1.g. Excellent design; preserve heritage
3.d. Share experience and research

Rules of Conduct
1. Inaccurate information—untruthfulness
7. Breach of confidentiality

Council Member Shares Opinion Privately About Upcoming Rezoning

You are the planning director of a city that has adopted zoning, and your department is charged with providing recommendations on rezoning applications. The city manager frequently calls you into his office to meet with city council members when they want to discuss the merits of upcoming rezoning applications to be voted on by the council. In such a meeting, regarding an application for rezoning to allow the expansion of an existing nursing home in your community, a council member suggests he will not vote in favor of the rezoning. You have not yet written your recommendation, but you do know there is strong support, and a Certificate of Need, for adding beds to the nursing home. Further, the applicant for the nursing home expansion has asked that you keep her informed of discussions and notify her of any political trends in the community that may affect the rezoning decision as it is processed. How do you handle the information you gained from the council member in the meeting with the city manager?

Commentary

The information the council member offered is not necessarily confidential, and rule of conduct 7 does not apply in this case. Rule 7 refers to use of confidential information by you for your own advantage or the advantage of a subsequent employer or client. In this case, you are contemplating releasing information to the applicant. A planner might interpret the applicant in this case to be a client; in such an instance rule 7 would then apply. However, other planners might not consider the applicant as a client. Your release of the information could be viewed by the council member as a breach of confidentiality, but it does not appear to violate rule of conduct 7. You should be able to confidently inform the applicant of the council member's views regarding the rezoning.

Relevant AICP Code Provision

Rules of Conduct
7.   Breach of confidentiality

56 Preapplication Meeting With Developer

*You are the assistant planning director for a county. The director assigns you to meet with a pro-
spective development applicant, who tells you of a preliminary proposal to build a new shopping
center. The developer discloses the types of tenants he expects to occupy the center if it is approved
and constructed. He wants preliminary feedback about the merits of the proposal, but asks that the
information be held in confidence because he has not closed on the property, and although one
tenant has agreed to occupy the proposed center, discussions with other prospective tenants are
ongoing and tentative. The applicant wants to know what is required to approve the development;
you determine that rezoning will not be necessary and that the applicant can proceed directly to
file development plans. Shortly after the meeting, a local newspaper calls and asks if there are any
pending development proposals in the community. How do you respond to the reporter?*

Commentary

You should not disclose the project to the media. The development preapplicant, who is your client in this case, has made
you privy to information he considers to be confidential (rule
7). It should be kept that way. There doesn't seem to be a
compelling, overriding public interest to you giving the information gained in the preapplication meeting to the media.
However, you need to phrase your response to the journalist
in such a way that you are not lying.

Nonetheless, in keeping the information confidential, are
you violating rule of conduct 1 by failing to provide "adequate" information on a planning issue? This is a case where
the situation does not constitute a "planning issue," in my view.

Relevant AICP Code Provision

Rules of Conduct
1. Inaccurate information—
   untruthfulness
7. Breach of confidentiality

57 Archaeological Site Discovered in Environmental Impact Review

A multidisciplinary consulting team is preparing an environmental impact review (EIR) for a large, complex project. Firm C is a planning consulting firm; and Firm H is an expert in historical, cultural, and archaeological resources. After an independent site visit, a member of Firm C discovers that there is an archaeological site on the property that is the subject of the EIR. The member of Firm C promptly notifies the project manager of Firm H of the archaeological find, but Firm H's project manager does not follow up or include reference to the archaeological find in the EIR report. Has the planner for Firm C satisfied her ethical obligation with the initial disclosure alone?

Commentary

The planner for Firm C who discovered the archaeological site has satisfied her ethical obligation, although due diligence would suggest that, in addition to notifying Firm H, she should have followed up with a phone call to discuss the matter and determine if it was properly documented in the report (1). However, the planner for Firm C is not an expert in archaeological resources and did the right thing to pass the information on to the consulting team member with the most expertise and the most direct responsibility. Besides, in defense of Firm C's planner, rule of conduct 15 indicates that she should not accept work beyond her own professional competence, and she passed on information to the team representative who had the expertise to decide. That expert may have looked at the site and concluded it was not an archaeological find. And it is not the proper role of Firm C's planner to direct Firm H to include the archaeological find in the EIR (rule 18).

Relevant AICP Code Provisions

Rules of Conduct

1. Inaccurate information— untruthfulness
15. Work beyond professional competence
18. Pressure: unsubstantiated findings

58 Consultant Without Prior Experience Pursues Work on a Fiscal Impact Study

A three-person consulting firm is struggling due to the economy and, as a result, is pursuing potential consulting projects on the margins of, or outside, its stated and documented specialties. The firm does not have any experience completing fiscal impact studies, but in preparing a proposal for work, the firm describes its work on other studies in a way that claims it has experience in fiscal impact analysis. Is this an ethical problem?

Commentary

The firm has overstepped the boundaries drawn in the AICP Code's rules of conduct. Consultants, especially hungry ones, would normally be expected to put their best spin on their credentials for a given work project. But in this case, the firm is making misleading claims and misstating qualifications, in violation of rules of conduct 11 and 12. And if the firm accepts the work beyond its professional competence without providing another competent professional who is acceptable to the client, it will also violate rule 15.

This is not to say that the firm would be precluded from bidding on the project, so long as it was truthful to the client about its qualifications in the area of fiscal impact analysis. A client could still decide to hire that firm, acknowledging that there would be a so-called learning curve.

Relevant AICP Code Provisions

Rules of Conduct

11. Solicitation via false claims; duress
12. Misstatement of one's qualifications
15. Work beyond professional competence

59 Invoicing for Work Not Yet Performed

You are a consulting planner. You receive a Request for Proposal, and it indicates that the project must be invoiced (not completed) within one month of consultant selection and contracting. Is it permissible to invoice for work not yet performed, to meet the client's deadline?

Commentary

It is permissible to invoice for work not yet performed. While it would not be ethical to bill the client if you do not intend to perform the work, that is not the same thing as entering into a specific agreement with the client to get paid in advance, with a promise to complete the work. This is a more difficult situation for the consultant than it may appear at first glance, however. This type of prepay situation may have a detrimental effect on your work performance. You will deposit the client's check knowing you are committed to doing the work in the future, but when the client needs the work done, your firm might be heavily engaged in other projects, and the prepaid work may take a lower priority. In such an instance, which is hypothetical but not unrealistic, you might risk violating rule of conduct 16 by not delivering promptly.

Relevant AICP Code Provisions

Rules of Conduct

16. Promptness of work required

SCENARIO 60
Unrealistic Work Deadline in Request for Proposal

A city's Request for Proposal (RFP) asks for a local comprehensive plan, and it specifies that the plan is to be prepared within a six-month time frame. You know the review process alone for the plan will take four months, leaving you only two months to accomplish public participation tasks and prepare the plan. You view it as impossible to undertake in that time frame. However, you know that other planning consultants are likely to bid on the project and in doing so suggest it can be done in the time frame, even if they know they cannot. What does your firm do? (Carolin, Gerhart-Fritz, and Weitz 2012)

Commentary

Contact the procurement officer for the RFP and raise your concerns in writing that the work cannot be undertaken within the specified time frame. Then ask for an extension of the schedule. If the RFP is amended by addendum to provide a workable amount of time to complete the work, you can bid. If the time frame is not extended, then you would violate rule of conduct 16 if you pursued the work and then were unable to deliver. Rule 12 reads: "We shall not misstate our education, experience, training, or any other facts which are relevant to our professional qualifications. It appears that such an action would violate rule 12, to the extent that you were misstating facts by saying that you could do the work within the time frame when you knew you could not.

Other consultants who want the job and may not be AICP members—or, potentially, unethical consultants who are AICP members—may bid on the project knowing that the time frame given to perform the work is unreasonable. If selected, they may start the work, then turn around almost immediately and request a change order extending the time frame. Once the job is under way, the city's project manager may be more likely to recognize that the time frame for completion of the project was overly aggressive. The ethical consultant knows this but does not succumb to that rationalization, because it infringes on rules of conduct and is inconsistent with aspirational principles of integrity.

Relevant AICP Code Provisions

Rules of Conduct

12. Misstatement of one's qualifications
16. Promptness of work required

Planner Writes Letter to the Editor

A planner employed by a city wrote a letter to the editor of the local newspaper, signing his name and home address, applauding and complimenting the county planning commission for recommending disapproval of a rezoning request that would allow expansion of industry in the county where his city employer is located. After reading the published letter to the editor, top elected city and county officials who support industrial expansion to grow the manufacturing job base in the county put pressure behind the scenes on the city planning director to fire the planner. How should the planning director respond? And was the letter written by the planner appropriate from an ethical perspective? (Based on Finkler 1971)

Commentary

Every planner has freedom of speech. In this scenario, the planner spoke out as an individual on a matter affecting his county of residence but outside the purview of the city, his employer. It is not appropriate for city and county leaders to put pressure on the city planning director to fire the planner for his outspokenness. While not bound by the AICP Code, the city and county elected officials should not be able to fire or threaten to fire any other member of the public who speaks against the rezoning but who does not work for the city. Hence they are not extending the planner fairness and evenhandedness (1.h). The director should respond to the suggestions that she fire the planner only after consulting applicable provisions of the city's personnel rules and consulting the city's human resources manager. We don't know what those rules would say, but they are unlikely to support the firing of the planner in this scenario.

However, there's an interesting potential twist of fate presented by rule of conduct 19. In writing the letter, wasn't the planner, in essence, participating in a "planning process," with a hearing and decision by the county governing body still to come? And, by signing the letter as a private citizen without acknowledging his employment in the city planning department, did the planner violate rule 19 by not disclosing the interests of his employer? Maybe the planner did not know what the city's official position was, or his employer may not have had an official written position on the issue of this rezoning.

The safe play, given the language of rule of conduct 19, would have been for the planner to acknowledge in the letter that he is employed as a planner for the city and that the opinions expressed in the letter are his own views, not those of the city. That would have gone a long way toward protecting the planner from an allegation that he violated rule 19. Meanwhile, if the city had no official written position on the rezoning case, the planner is probably not susceptible to

Relevant AICP Code Provisions

Principles to Which We Aspire

1.h. Deal fairly and evenhandedly

Rules of Conduct

19. Concealment of interest/
    failure to disclose

a charge of violating rule 19. The planner cannot guess the city's position, or extrapolate from one or more statements by elected officials, that there is official support for the rezoning.

For Further Discussion

What if the planning director sends a letter to the city and county elected officials stating that there are no grounds to fire the planner, and the officials threaten that the city council can fire the planning director—for virtually any reason, because she is appointed—if she doesn't find a way to justify firing the planner?

62 City Attorney Conflict

You are a consulting planner who works for a city doing zoning administration. The city attorney is also a real estate attorney. You have observed that the city attorney frequently has private real estate clients. In cases of conflict between a private real estate client's interest and the city's, this attorney chooses the interests of the private real estate client to the detriment of the city, whom he is also charged with representing. The city attorney also has many political connections in city government, and you believe he is likely to retaliate if you raise the issue publicly. As a certified planner witnessing this, what do you do? (Carolin, Gerhart-Fritz, and Weitz 2012)

Commentary

What the city attorney is doing is an unethical conflict of interest and may be against the law. If you believe that it is in the public interest that the city not be hurt by the city attorney's conflict (1 and 2), or if it is otherwise ruled as such, rule of conduct 2 would apply, and you should not in my view continue with your work for the city lest you violate that rule. You need to have solid proof to blow the whistle on the city attorney, however, and if you show any recklessness in that regard, you could possibly violate rule of conduct 10. You may not be able to provide diligent work for the client under the circumstances of the city attorney's conflict; if so, a violation of rule 16 could be evident. Rule of conduct 19 appears to make it a requirement that you either end the client-consultant relationship or blow the whistle on the city attorney, because the ethical planner must disclose that the interests of the city are being violated by the city's own attorney, who is supposed to be looking after the city's interest.

With all of that said, the power of ethics may not be strong enough in this instance to motivate you to blow the whistle. You may have your livelihood to consider and, despite the ethical calls to the contrary, feel that you are not in a position to blow the whistle or quit working for that client.

Relevant AICP Code Provisions

Principles to Which We Aspire

1. (preamble). Allegiance to public interest
2. (preamble). Competent performance

Rules of Conduct

2. Illegal or unethical conduct
10. Misrepresentation of others' qualifications
16. Promptness of work required
19. Concealment of interest/ failure to disclose

63

Use of Primary Employer's Equipment for Consulting Assignment

You are a transportation planning manager employed by a state transportation agency. In the past you have done consulting work for private developers and occasionally for local governments, with the express, written approval of your supervisor in state government. Now you have contracted with a local government to do a highway corridor plan, and you need to complete traffic counts for the corridor. You don't own vehicle-trip-counting equipment, and your consulting contract budget did not provide for you to purchase it. Your primary employer, the state transportation agency, has the equipment, which is currently not in use. Do you avail yourself of the state's equipment for the consulting project?

Commentary

There is no conceivable public interest in using state equipment for private gain. If you availed yourself of the state equipment, you would be using your power of office to gain access to public equipment to be used for private gain. Therefore, it would be a conflict of interest (2.c). Using the equipment would most likely violate rule of conduct 14.

If you used the equipment, you would create ethical issues with both your primary employer and the consulting client. Acting as a consultant, you should anticipate that certain equipment is needed and budget for it in the project. You would be wrong to use the equipment because you would have accepted work for a fee that cannot be performed except in circumstances different from those disclosed to the local government client (rule 16). Similarly, if you solicited the local government client without disclosing the use of state equipment, then it would appear you violated rule 11, to the extent that your assurances were false or misleading.

Even the negotiation of a consulting contract with the predetermination that you will be using state equipment, with or without permission, is improper. Such a circumstance could be interpreted as a misstatement of qualifications to the consulting client and could rise to the level of a violation of rule 12. Your use of public equipment for private gain would also appear to violate rule 5.

You have permission to consult, consistent with rule of conduct 4. However, without written permission to use the state-owned equipment for a private consulting project, you have no authority to use the equipment, and it would be improper to do so. You have accepted an assignment and may violate rule of conduct 2 if you are unable to perform the work or can complete it only by borrowing state equipment that you are not authorized to use.

Even if permission were granted, it would not be permissible for you to use the state equipment for private work. State

Relevant AICP Code Provisions

Principles to Which We Aspire

2.c. Avoid appearance of conflict of interest

3.a. Enhance professional integrity

Rules of Conduct

2. Illegal or unethical conduct
4. Outside employment ("moon lighting")
5. Acceptance of gifts or advantage
11. Solicitation via false claims; duress
12. Misstatement of one's qualifications
14. Official power used for advantage
16. Promptness of work required
25. Deliberate, wrongful act

equipment cannot be used for private gain. To do so would reflect adversely on professional fitness (rule 25). The equipment may be subject to wear and tear, and it could become broken, lost, stolen, or destroyed. Even if you replaced the equipment rather promptly after it was destroyed or damaged, the agency might not have immediate access to that equipment, something it certainly deserves by virtue of its ownership.

SCENARIO 64

Developer and Public-Sector Planner Have Lunch Together

A developer who has a planned unit development (PUD) proposal pending in the city where you are a planner invites you to join her for lunch. It is lunchtime, you are hungry, and you think nothing of it; the developer did not say she would pay for lunch. You make a split-second decision to go along with her. You sit down in a local cafe, and the developer begins to cite reasons why the PUD will be good for the city and why the local planning staff, of which you are a part, should wholeheartedly support the development when it comes up for recommendation by the planning commission and decision by the city council. The cafe is crowded, and people you recognize are within hearing distance of your table. The developer grabs the check and says she is in a hurry to make an appointment. What do you do?

Commentary

Decline the developer's offer to pay for lunch, even if you have to run to catch up with her. In this scenario, you have no time to think; you have to act immediately. Inaction is a decision also, because the result of inaction will be that the developer pays for lunch. Your instantaneous decision to go to lunch with the developer should be second-guessed. Learn from your mistake and be more wary of these invitations in the future. It does not matter whether people are within hearing distance and can observe you with the developer; the ethical planning practitioner would act ethically whether being observed or not. Moreover, the ethical planner would have declined the invitation in the first place.

You should avoid this type of situation because it involves many instances of unethical conduct. It is not fair to others in the upcoming public hearing on the PUD to gather information and open yourself up to being persuaded by the developer outside the context of the legal process (1.h). In some states, this may be considered ex parte contact or communication that, by law, would have to be disclosed. Independent professional judgment could be compromised (2.a). It sounds like a conflict of interest to anyone who overheard the conversation (2.c). When the perception of a conflict arises with regard to a planner's action, the integrity of the profession is not protected or at least is certainly not enhanced (3.a).

Moving next to the three rules of conduct that appear applicable, if you allow the developer to pay for your lunch, it is reasonably clear the developer is interested in the lunch discussion because of your public role—that is, the discussion is definitely related to your public employment. This violates rule of conduct 5. Similarly, the lunch violates rules 8 and 14, because there was no disclosure of the lunch, and, as the conversation was one-sided from developer to planner, the lunch cannot be rationalized as being "in the public interest."

Relevant AICP Code Provisions

Principles to Which We Aspire
1.h. Deal fairly and evenhandedly
2.a. Exercise independent judgment
2.c. Avoid appearance of conflict of interest
3.a. Enhance professional integrity

Rules of Conduct
5. Acceptance of gifts or advantage
8. Private communication (public)
14. Official power used for advantage

During the lunch, you engaged in private communication with the developer as a participant in a planning process (the development review). You should not do that if the discussion relates to a matter over which you have influence—that is, if you will provide a written recommendation to the planning commission or the governing body (rule 8). A strict reading of rule 8 would suggest that it may be inapplicable, because you do not have "authority to make a binding, final determination." Yet, if you do have final authority to make a decision about what to recommend, then there is at least some chance that the lunch violates the spirit of rule of conduct rule 8. This is a case where you should interpret rules of conduct broadly, beyond the strict situational constraints the code articulates. The ethical planning practitioner does not rationalize away the rules by finding that circumstances are slightly different or that the strict construction of rules of conduct renders the rules inapplicable.

65   Valuables Found on Pending Development Site

You are a staff planner for a county planning and development office. You are assigned an up-coming development plan review and routinely visit development sites for field reconnaissance prior to reviewing development plans. You are alone and visit such a site, which has already been cleared for development after proper permits have been obtained. While walking the site, you discover that the heavy machinery has unearthed a ceramic crock full of jewelry and cash. What do you do?

Commentary

Secure the jewelry and cash, return them to your office, and immediately bring them to the attention of your supervisor and others as necessary. They need to be returned to the property owner (the developer), even if the developer did not place the valuables there and was not aware of their existence (5). Why do you tell more than one person? So that your supervisor will resist any temptation to keep the valuables without reporting them, possibly without your knowledge, or to suggest that you both should keep quiet and split the valuables for your own advantage. Let the higher authorities of government take it from there, with the understanding that they will return the valuables to the developer. Remember, you would have never found the valuables in the first place if you were not at the site on official county business.

Relevant AICP Code Provision

Rules of Conduct

5.   Acceptance of gifts or advantage

Publication of Client's Report

You are a consulting planner and have just finished a report for a public-sector client. The client has found the report satisfactory, you have been paid, and the contractual arrangements have been satisfied. Reading the AICP Code, you note that certified planners are supposed to share experiences, so you modify the client's report and seek publication of the modified work. You will receive an honorarium for the publication. Is it ethical for you to accept the additional remuneration for work you have already been paid for and that is really your client's work?

Commentary

The client bought and paid for the report. It remains the client's product. Some planners might legitimately claim the right to retain the intellectual property, and even aspire to share the results of experience and research when such opportunities arise (3.d). However, those considerations are not strong enough to overcome rule of conduct 5, which indicates that we cannot accept a rebate from "anyone other than our public employer"—in this case, an honorarium from a publisher—if it is "perceived as related to our public office or employment." The honorarium would be perceived that way, because the client paid for the report, and you wrote the report while being employed by that client.

This scenario actually happened to me. I informed the client that I had the opportunity to publish the client's report and that successful publication would result in an honorarium. Despite any value I added in rewriting the report to broaden its individual state perspective for a national audience, I offered the honorarium to the client. The client declined the honorarium and authorized me to keep it, so I did.

For Further Discussion

Did I act unethically in accepting the honorarium, even though the employer explicitly approved? Is acceptance of the honorarium still a violation of the strict dictates of rule of conduct 5? After all, rule 5 does not say "unless your client agrees." In retrospect, with sufficient time before the honorarium was processed and accepted, wouldn't it have been more prudent for me to seek formal or informal advice from the Ethics Officer, in light of this lingering doubt? Should consultants who contemplate publishing results from client projects include a provision in their agreement addressing the terms on which such publication is acceptable?

Relevant AICP Code Provisions

Principles to Which We Aspire

3.d. Share experience and research

Rules of Conduct

5. Acceptance of gifts or advantage

67 Public Funds Used to Clean Clothing

You are a government planner. While on a business trip, you use public funds to clean your clothing. Is this advisable? (Based on Wachs 1985)

Commentary

The answer depends on exactly which clothes you had cleaned. It would seem appropriate to use public funds to clean an official uniform or personal clothes that met acceptable standards for dress for the employer if the clothes were soiled while you were on the business trip and no other suitable clothes were available. It would not be appropriate to clean clothing unrelated to the business trip or if other appropriate clothes were available on the business trip. If you are still in doubt as to the appropriateness of using public funds for cleaning clothes, you could seek your employer's permission for the expenditure. If one interprets "power of any office" to include the discretionary power of the purse, deliberate use of government funds for private purposes would violate rule of conduct 14 and may violate rule 25. Misuse of public funds would not reflect positively on professional fitness or protect the integrity of the profession.

Relevant AICP Code Provisions

Rules of Conduct

14. Official power used for advantage
25. Deliberate, wrongful act

68 Proposal to Travel for Training

A public-sector planner, who is an AICP member, submits a request to travel to a state conference, and his justification for attending is that he needs continuing education maintenance credits to remain in good standing with AICP. The planner is particularly interested in the location of the state conference because a longtime friend lives in that city, plus a minor league baseball team is in town and scheduled to play during one of the evenings of the conference. The planner does not disclose that there are web-based training programs available that are either free or less costly when compared with the travel dollars required to attend the state conference. Is this unethical?

Commentary

This scenario is not about a "planning process" and does not relate to "information on planning issues." Therefore, an argument can be made that rules of conduct 1 and 19 do not apply. However, read together, one might consider the intent of these rules more broadly. The planner has not necessarily misstated anything in asking the employer for permission to travel, hence rule 12 does not appear to be violated either. But he has not mentioned the alternative: that he could meet training requirements by another means that does not cost the government travel money. If the planner presented the conference as the only training available that would meet the requirement for maintaining his AICP certification, when in fact a less expensive option was available, that might arguably violate rule 12.

Of most concern is rule of conduct 14. It is not in the public interest that the planner gets to see his friend and attend an out-of-town minor league baseball game. The planner appears to be motivated by private gain, so he may have violated rule14, because the proposed travel request is not public knowledge. Though his request is cloaked with the valid purpose of continuing education (3.h), the planner appears to be attempting to use the power of public office—and spending authority—for a supplemental private advantage or gain. Is the planner obligated to inform the supervisor that a less costly alternative is available?

While some planners might not give this situation much ethical consideration, the ethical planning practitioner would disclose all possible methods of receiving the mandatory continuing education credits necessary to maintain the AICP credential, along with his desire to attend the training event, which requires travel funds, and let the supervisor decide. An ethical planner would see the self-interest associated with his travel request—beyond the legitimate justification of continuing education—and not propose the trip without offering to pay for some or all of the travel costs himself.

Relevant AICP Code Provisions

Principles to Which We Aspire

3.h. Enhance education and training

Rules of Conduct

1. Inaccurate information—untruthfulness
12. Misstatement of one's qualifications
14. Official power used for advantage
19. Concealment of interest/failure to disclose

69 Public Planners Offered Free, Hard-to-Get Tickets

You are a planner for a jurisdiction that is home to a popular college football team. The university offers several members of the planning staff tickets to a sold-out game. Recognizing the conflict, your boss and colleagues decide to pay for their tickets, thus obviating the question of whether or not the tickets were a gift. Is there still an ethical conflict? (Based on APA 2012)

Commentary

This type of courting of influence may seem routine and not a violation of ethics. Universities give away tickets for many reasons and purposes, and they might do so routinely, even for sold-out games. Some may view the tickets as a simple, appropriate perk of the job. At first glance, there doesn't seem to be any harm to anyone, except perhaps the people who might have otherwise acquired the tickets. Maybe there is no harm, but an ethics code subjects professionals to a different set of rules which prevent them from accepting the tickets.

The acceptance of the tickets, if made publicly known, could easily create the appearance of a conflict of interest, contrary to principle 2.c. In my view, this situation is a clear and direct violation of rule of conduct 5 of the AICP Code, so ethical planners would not have done so. Accepting the tickets appears to violate rule 14, because the tickets were offered to public planners, and their acceptance of the tickets would not normally be a matter of public knowledge and certainly cannot be rationalized as being in the public interest.

Accepting the tickets is a violation of rule of conduct 8 if university officials attend the game alongside the planners and discuss, or want to discuss, a pending development decision for which the public planners have final authority, even if there was no agency rule, procedure, or custom that addresses this type of behavior. In the same vein, accepting the tickets probably violates rule 9, because it is not customary or customarily appropriate to discuss such matters at a sporting event.

A planner who engages in such a discussion of a pending development approval may fall into further unethical behavior via rule of conduct 13. It is easy to foresee a situation where a planner, in exchange for the favor of receiving the tickets, responds: "I'll talk to the director about the reasons you have given for our department to approve the development proposal."

Rule of conduct 5 makes accepting the tickets clearly unethical; rule 14 also renders the situation unethical; and rules 8 and 9 raise more ethical concerns. Beyond these rules, the question of ethical conflict depends on what behavior the university officials expect from the planners in terms of their public roles. If you believe that the tickets are offered to you because

Relevant AICP Code Provisions

Principles to Which We Aspire
2.c. Avoid appearance of conflict
     of interest

Rules of Conduct
5. Acceptance of gifts or advantage
8. Private communication (public)
9. Private communication (other)
13. Influence via improper means
14. Official power used for
     advantage
25. Deliberate, wrongful act

you are in an official position, which appears obvious from the scenario, you must ask what official benefit your employer derives, or expects to derive, by accepting the tickets. Does the university have frequent business with your department and make requests for the review and approval of site plans, building permits, design review, certificates of occupancy, and so forth? It may be difficult to find an official connection between the private benefit of attending a sporting event, presumably as a private person, and your official capacity as a professional planner working for a local government. Is there some reason why you would need to attend the game in an official capacity? Almost surely not, and even asking that question may represent an intent to accept and make up an excuse in order to rationalize accepting a private benefit as a public planner. It is private gain or advantage, and you must say no.

Even though the planners have paid for their tickets, there is still a potential benefit gained by the planners from the university, because the game is sold out and tickets are not available. Paying for the tickets still leaves the planners with the need to acknowledge the favor of getting to see a game they would not otherwise have been able to see in person. Therefore, even paying for the tickets is, in my view, still a violation of rule 5 and probably rule 14.

Another way of viewing the issue, independent of specific rules, is to consider how comfortable the planners would be with the decision to accept the tickets if the newspaper ran an exposé about how staff in the planning department accepted tickets to a sold-out football game. It is not too hard to imagine that a neighborhood group opposed to the university's intended expansion into its subdivision would see the university's ticket offer as courting favor with public planners outside the planning process but toward its objective of university expansion. It is hard to imagine a way to rationalize the planners' acceptance of the tickets so that the public would still see them as good planners. Public knowledge of the planners' acceptance of the tickets could "reflect adversely on our professional fitness," in violation of rule of conduct 25, because it could be considered to be a deliberate wrongful act to accept the ticket.

In conclusion, the acceptance and use of the tickets constitute direct personal gain. An ethical planner will steer clear of such situations. In addition to violating enforceable rules, acceptance of the tickets does not reflect the "high standards of professional integrity" expected via the aspirational principles of the AICP Code. It does not "protect," and it certainly does not "enhance," the integrity of our profession. Because other community groups and individuals cannot curry the same favor as the university can, the planners' acceptance of the tickets is not consistent with the aspirational principle that "Those of us who are public officials or employees shall also deal evenhandedly with all planning process participants"—whether this is considered a planning process or not. Acceptance of the tickets may compromise, or be seen to compromise, the planners' ability to "exercise independent professional judgment on behalf of our clients and employers," because, consciously or not, the planners will remember enjoying the game in person, and that memory may influence their future decision making.

70 Consultant Invites Potential Clients to Dinner

A private consultant, who is an AICP member, invites potential clients, including AICP members who work in the public sector, to various dinners over time to discuss potential contracts and future work. Is this ethical or unethical? (Based on APA 2012)

Commentary

APA (2012, 21) answered the question succinctly: "It is not unethical to discuss contracts generally, your firm's interests, or your capabilities. If you are actively backing a specific contract, it would not be appropriate." Many consultants routinely offer potential clients free dinners, and for the planning consultant not to do so may place her at a competitive disadvantage. But as an AICP member, she needs to consider the ethical consequences of her actions, although other consultants may not be inclined to do so.

The ethics of the AICP public planners who are the consultant's potential clients and attend the dinners also need to be evaluated. The consultant is not a public official or a public employee; therefore, it would seem that rule of conduct 5 does not apply to her. However, it would probably be a violation of rule 5 for public planners to accept the dinners, because acceptance would most likely and appropriately be perceived as related to their offices or positions. Similarly, if a public planner who is an AICP member attends the dinners, and if he has final authority to hire that consultant for a given project, he most likely violates competitive procurement processes of the city, in potential violation of rule of conduct 8. Though not specifically evident in this scenario, such a situation also opens up the planning consultant to potential violations of rules of conduct 11, 12, and, in her solicitation of work, rule 13. When the behavior could potentially lead to violations of rules of conduct in the future, the ethical planning practitioner—whether a private consultant or a public-sector planner as potential client—steers away from such activities.

Relevant AICP Code Provisions

Rules of Conduct

5. Acceptance of gifts or advantage
8. Private communication (public)
11. Solicitation via false claims; duress
12. Misstatement of one's qualifications
13. Influence via improper means

SCENARIO 71 — Real Estate Investment Along Proposed New Highway

You are a planner working for a state transportation agency. You participated in the preparation of medium-range (10-year) state plans, which include a project to build a new state highway from Point A to Point B. You have an opportunity to invest in real estate along the proposed route of the new state highway. Can you invest in real estate along the route and still fulfill your ethical obligations?

Commentary

You probably cannot invest and still fulfill your ethical obligations. The opportunity to invest is an advantage accruing to you as a result of your public position. Together, rule of conduct 14 and principle 2.c suggest that investing could be perceived as a conflict of interest. At issue is whether you, as a potential investor, would be perceived to be receiving some advantage from your public employment role (5) or to be using information derived from your public position to obtain a special advantage that is not a matter of public knowledge and not in the public interest (14). If you contemplate the investment opportunity before the plan is completed and publicly available, you will violate rule of conduct 6, which, in these circumstances, requires you to disclose your intent to invest and seek consent of your employer. On top of these rule considerations, a variety of ethical principles (including 3.a) could be cited against this type of investment.

For Further Discussion

Does it make a difference if the state plans are already adopted, and thus on public record, or merely pending?

Relevant AICP Code Provisions

Principles to Which We Aspire

2.c. Avoid appearance of conflict of interest

3.a. Enhance professional integrity

Rules of Conduct

5. Acceptance of gifts or advantage
6. Personal or financial gain
14. Official power used for advantage

72 Influencing Land-Use Plan Designation for Real Property You Own

You are an AICP planner and an elected council member in a small town. The town has authority to adopt zoning but has never adopted a zoning ordinance. Hence, there are no current land-use restrictions. You own and live in a house along a state highway running through the center of the town—that is, on Main Street, both literally and figuratively. You believe that during the planning horizon, the houses along the state route, including yours, may be converted to, or replaced by, offices and commercial uses. You would like to maximize the value of your home for resale. You have the opportunity to review a land-use plan prepared by a consultant for the city, which shows your property and the others along the highway corridor as remaining single-family residential during the 20-year planning horizon. Can you ethically recommend to the consultant that she change the land-use designation of your property and all of the houses along the highway corridor from residential to office or commercial in the land-use plan?

Commentary

You could convert your property to office use in the present day, given that there are no zoning restrictions, notwithstanding any potential future plan or zoning ordinance. Hence, if you are to advocate for anything in this scenario, it would be to (1) extend certain property rights enjoyed now into the future; or (2) have the land-use plan reflect what you think is in the best interests of not only yourself but also other property owners along the main highway.

The chief concern would probably come from an inquiring public or media who view these circumstances as a conflict of interest (2.c). Is there a conflict of interest inherent in your professional planning role? Arguably not, because you are not the one preparing the plan. Furthermore, in your role as council member, you have authority to vote on the adoption of the land-use plan. Could the perceived conflict of interest be explained away by the observation that the properties are not zoned, and thus your intent could be accomplished in the present day, never mind what a future nonbinding plan might show? Or is this just personal rationalization and irrelevant (14)?

It seems to me that you could act as contemplated without violating the AICP Code. However, consider how potentially uncomfortable it may be for you to defend your position if it were raised in public. The ethics of the situation may be decided most directly by the question of whether you are acting out of personal interest in real property (which is possibly unethical); or whether legitimate public interests (that is, the interests of multiple property owners plus the town) are served by your advocacy (which is possibly ethical).

Still, I think the contemplated behavior is not necessarily discouraged by the AICP Code, given that you are acting

Relevant AICP Code Provisions

Principles to Which We Aspire

2.c. Avoid appearance of conflict of interest

Rules of Conduct

14. Official power used for advantage

in a personal and community capacity, not in a professional planning role.

For Further Discussion

An interesting question is whether planners in elected positions are required to maintain their professional ethics. Do planners in elected positions separate and then downplay considerations of professional ethics when the decisions are made by elected officials, and where nothing involves their own work as planning professionals? Can professional planners who are also elected officials discard the AICP Code while acting in the capacity of an elected official, or do obligations of professional planners still follow them when they are acting in extraprofessional roles?

73 Inspector/Planner Promotes His Own Inspection Company

The town planner in a small town is also the town's building inspector. The inspector/planner also maintains a home inspection company alongside his public-sector job. In interacting with the public, the inspector/planner frequently suggests to applicants that his company can provide home inspections when needed for resales. Is this an ethical conflict?

Commentary

This practice is not at all ethical. If the inspector/planner is an AICP member, he is potentially subject to complaints involving multiple infractions of the AICP Code's rules of conduct. If the inspector/planner doesn't have permission from his town to engage in the inspection company's business, rule of conduct 4 is violated. Similarly, without permission from the town to engage in the business, there is personal gain to the inspector/planner, which violates rule 6. Because the inspector/planner is soliciting clients for his inspection company while engaged in the town's business, he is taking advantage of opportunities to come into contact with potential customers whom he would not encounter unless he was the town's employee, thus violating rule 5. And the exposure the inspector/planner receives from interaction with people on the job equates to using town employment to obtain special advantage that is not in the public interest, thus violating rule 14.

An ethics notice published by APA in the September 2014 edition of *Practicing Planner* provides an official determination in a similar situation. A planner was found by the Ethics Officer to be in violation rules 4, 5, and 6 of the AICP Code because, without written permission from his local government employer, he was paid for the use of his landscape contractor license and license number on landscape plans submitted to the local government for which he was employed. In the same notice, AICP reminds all planners that "full disclosure and written permission from one's employer is a code requirement before undertaking outside employment related to planning. Additionally, receiving compensation for outside work 'that may be perceived as related to our public office or employment' is strictly prohibited regardless of permission."

Relevant AICP Code Provisions

Rules of Conduct

4. Outside employment ("moonlighting")
5. Acceptance of gifts or advantage
6. Personal or financial gain
14. Official power used for advantage

SCENARIO

74 Planner Evaluates Prior Employee for Employment Elsewhere

Planner A, an AICP member, is a former public-sector planning director and is now a private-sector planner. He has been asked, and has agreed, to serve on a personnel review and selection committee for a local government's planning director position. In reviewing the applications, Planner A notices that one of the applicants, Planner B, was a planner working under him when he was a planning director. Planner B had filed a complaint and charge of ethical misconduct with AICP against Planner A. Remembering this, Planner A recommends against Planner B for the planning director position and points out details to the rest of the selection committee about her poor performance while working with the agency Planner A directed. What are the ethical implications of Planner A's actions?

Commentary

Because of rule of conduct 22, planner A cannot retaliate against Planner B for her previous filing of an ethics complaint against Planner A. It is not evident in this scenario whether Planner A has misrepresented the qualifications of Planner B, but if so, he has violated rule of conduct 10.

Relevant AICP Code Provisions

Rules of Conduct

10. Misrepresentation of others' qualifications
22. Retaliation for misconduct charge

Planning Director Disciplines Junior Planner

Planner A, a planner in a county, filed a complaint and charge of ethical misconduct under the AICP Code against his supervisor, Planner B, the county planning director, who is an AICP member. The charge is currently under investigation. Planner B has been watching Planner A's on-the-job performance carefully. As soon as she can reasonably justify it, Planner B threatens to fire Planner A for poor job performance and also threatens to file an ethics charge against him with AICP for alleged unethical behavior. Is this unethical conduct?

Commentary

Planner B's actions are unethical, because they violate two rules of conduct of the AICP Code. Rule 22 is violated by Planner B with the threat to file an ethics charge. And if Planner B's actions are motivated by revenge against Planner A, a violation of rule 22 exists. If Planner B constructs frivolous evidence, she violates rule 24.

Relevant AICP Code Provisions

Rules of Conduct

22. Retaliation for misconduct charge
24. No frivolous ethics charge

76 Planner Responds to AICP Ethics Charge of Misconduct

Planner A has been charged with ethical misconduct and is currently the subject of an AICP investigation for violation of the AICP Code. The central issue in the complaint is that Planner A published information prepared by a planning consultant, Planner B, in a journal article, and that Planner A claimed it was his own work without any reference to the original source. Planner A is directed by the Ethics Officer to submit certain documents that are relevant to the ethics complaint, including the original work by Planner B that was cited in the ethics complaint. Planner A finds two versions of Planner B's work on his computer: the final version, which contains the information that Planner A allegedly used without permission and proper citation; and a draft, which does not contain the information. Planner A provides the draft version of the report to the Ethics Officer. Is this unethical conduct?

Commentary

Planner A has withheld information from the Ethics Officer. This behavior is unethical, because it violates rule of conduct 21.

Relevant AICP Code Provision

Rules of Conduct

21. Cooperation in AICP investigation

INTERPRETATIONS AND CONCLUSIONS

In this final part, I suggest some interpretations of the AICP Code and offer conclusions.

Suggested Interpretations of the Code

The code includes a number of key phrases but does not provide definitions except for "serious crime." The decision not to provide definitions in the AICP Code is, for the most part, intentional, because definitions and interpretations—of "the public interest," for example—will depend on the specific context and will most likely change from one context to another, as well as evolve over time. Listed in this section are several instances where the AICP Code, strictly construed, limits significantly the context in which the rule applies. The ethical planning practitioner will examine ways in which a rule of conduct might be deemed applicable even if a plausible argument could be made that a strict interpretation of the rule would render it inapplicable.

Accept an assignment
This phrase in the AICP Code—used in principle 2.c and rules of conduct 2 and 3, and its variation, "accept work," as used in rule 16, should be broadly construed to mean not only accepting an assignment but also "continuing an assignment." A planner may have already been engaged in a given assignment when an ethical issue arises. The ethical planning practitioner will not continue working on an assignment that requires actions inconsistent with the AICP Code.

Adequate information
The aspiration to provide adequate information (principle 1.d and rule of conduct 1) should be interpreted as an aspiration to provide "complete" information, with no omissions. Deliberately omitting information could be considered a violation of rule of conduct 1 and aspirational principle 1.d, even though the term "complete" does not appear in the applicable code provisions. Exclusion of certain information should be considered inconsistent with these code provisions, in my view.

Authority to make a binding, final determination
A planner who has authority to make a formal recommendation should construe rule of conduct 8 to be applicable, even though the strict context would suggest that a formal recommendation is clearly not a "binding, final determination."

Decision makers
The provision of rule of conduct 19 that planners shall not engage in discussions with "decision makers" in a manner prohibited by rules, procedures, or custom might be broadened to include private discussions with certain groups. To exclude private groups from this code construct would assume that they have no power to make relevant decisions or at least no ability to influence such decisions.

Employment
When considering whether a given action or activity is a conflict of interest, interpret the term "employment," as used in rule of conduct 4, to include elected positions. Further, it may be extended to appointed positions, even if they do not come with remuneration. Also, rule 4, which applies to "salaried" employees, should be considered more broadly applicable to any "contracted" employee or consultant. Moreover, in other places, the AICP Code uses broader terms—"professional services we perform" (2.b) and "services to be performed" (rule 2)—which may be applied in additional contexts.

Other professionals
"Other professionals," as used in rule of conduct 10, should be interpreted to include planning professionals and participants in all other professions.

Planning issues
The phrase "planning issues" appears in rule of conduct 1. Planners engaged in administrative decision making on a zoning recommendation or grant proposal may conclude that such activities are not "planning issues." "Planning issues" are broad and should be interpreted to include instances outside the periphery of actual planning processes. The spirit of the AICP Code, in my view, would suggest that this rule of conduct should be applied broadly and thoroughly.

Planning process
This phrase appears in principle 1.h and rules of conduct 8, 9, and 19. Zoning and development code administration, as well as other facets of planners' work, should be broadly interpreted to be within the realm of a "planning process" for purposes of the AICP Code's rules of conduct. Similarly, "planning process participants" should, by extension, be broadly construed to apply to people making decisions involving administrative discretion as well as anyone engaged in any other activities that involve planners but lie outside the mainstream of planning processes. The context of the "planning process" might even be broadened to include personnel matters. Also, litigation after a rezoning decision could conceivably be considered a continuation of the planning process. The ethical planning practitioner will critically contemplate when the planning process starts and ends, extending the timing beyond the strict situation at hand. Hearings and debates on a zoning decision could reasonably be considered a planning process, in my view. I foresee circumstances where it could be appropriate to extend the term "planning process" even to a decision about whether to attend a training event. Finally, how does one treat an action by a certified planner that technically falls outside the traditionally accepted notion of a "planning process"—for example, that takes place in the political environment of an elected official?

Solicit prospective clients or employment
This provision in rule of conduct 11 should be interpreted as applying not only to private planning consultants but to public- and nonprofit-sector planners who are trying to conduct consulting assignments or seek other gain.

Conclusions

This book, which focuses on the applicability of the AICP Code of Ethics and Professional Conduct, approaches questions of ethics in planning practice using a mostly "legalistic" approach, at least initially. My central conclusion is this: Practicing planners will almost always gain a satisfactory answer to an ethics question by applying a legalistic perspective—that is, by systematically examining the AICP Code and applicable laws and rules. The ethical planning practitioner achieves this by rigorously analyzing how each and every aspirational principle and rule of conduct, as well as applicable laws and rules, may apply to a given ethics question.

Many planners take a legalistic approach to ethics at the outset. After all, when we act, the greatest threat is that our activities may be illegal according to local or state laws. One of the first questions a planner is likely to ask is whether his or her activities broke the law. Close behind that first question, the ethical planning practitioner will ask if there is a rule of conduct in the AICP Code that governs the matter or specifically indicates whether an activity is unethical and thus disallowed.

Every AICP planner should want to stay out of trouble with the law and avoid behaving in an unethical way that is subject to scrutiny by the professional institute's enforcement arm. A legalistic approach is a safe and practical way to achieve those goals and is perhaps the best place for planners to start. Taking a legalistic approach helps us to meet the biggest need of all planners: to protect our livelihoods—that is, self-interest—while doing our jobs ethically.

There are limits to a purely legalistic approach to ethics, and therefore, there are some clear limits to the narrow focus on the AICP Code in this book. Laws cannot cover every type of misbehavior that may be contemplated. Enforceable rules of conduct must maintain some general applicability and therefore must sometimes be vague in practical application. This is evident in the prior section, which shows how there is much room for planners to interpret the strict dictates of the AICP Code.

A potential big danger of the legalistic approach to ethics is that it could lead to narrow, impoverished views of ethics in planning (Howe 1994). The fact that an action is legal does not mean it is morally permissible to take that action (Barrett 2001). In other words, laws do not include moral and ethical statements. Bolan (1983) makes a similar point in his observation that codes of conduct "offer a false sense of security and obscure the subtle, tacit and unstated norms that are often instrumental in guiding action."

I have distilled some key points from Howe (1994) and my own thoughts into this set of suggested best practices:

Extend ethical values to non-AICP members. Do not discard a given ethical issue simply because the person acting unethically is not an AICP member. APA Ethical Principles in Planning (1992) apply to all planners, whether they are members of APA or not. And those principles are, in many ways, similar to the content of the AICP Code.

Rely on public processes to infuse legitimacy. Planners should consider how open a process is in arriving at a public decision. Accountability should take precedence over a planner's own idea of the public interest if the decision is made in an open process. Do not substitute your own conception of the public interest for a notion of the public interest that is arrived at through an open and fair public process. Actions that would violate duties of justice should be resisted and should not be justified by appeals to serving the public interest (Howe 1994).

Be wary of perceptions of special advantage. Be wary of situations where others could perceive that you are obtaining a special advantage from a position or appointment. Think more deeply about how conflicts of interest could surface. Anticipate conflicts and responses, and write them into a conflict-of-interest management plan.

Do not condone the conflicts of interest of others. Do not acquiesce to another person's conflict of interest, because knowingly letting such a conflict continue without dissenting is inconsistent with the AICP Code. Acquiescence means you are tacitly confirming and condoning that unethical behavior by another person.

Consider the consequences of dissent and covert action. Consider whether your ethical principles and your cause are worth the fight, and whether it is prudent for you to rock the boat. Consider whether letting the issue slide will allow you more influence in the long run. The option of acting covertly should be viewed with suspicion. Go underground only if you are prepared to face the consequences.

Disseminate information widely. If information is appropriate for dissemination to one person or group of persons, then it is appropriate to distribute it broadly to others, even if they are not sympathetic to your cause.

Employ avoidance strategies. To relieve political pressure, sidestep any discussions with elected officials outside the public planning and public hearing processes, if possible. Ask that elected officials raise issues in public forums, rather than privately and individually with you.

Act on opportunities to pursue social goals. Recognize, and act on, opportunities to advance social justice.

When in doubt, seek permission. When in doubt or in an ethical gray area, seek permission to engage in the contemplated activity.

Be careful where you choose to invest. Avoid investment opportunities that have even a remote relation to your official position or are within the jurisdiction in which you work.

Treat younger planners with delicacy. If you are a director, when a junior planner disagrees with your position, spend time educating the younger planner on why you have arrived at your decision. Make sure you can prove any allegations of misconduct against a younger planner. Help young planners understand their errors and forgive them for first offenses.

The Ethical Planning Practitioner
Building on Steinberg and Austern (1990) and Barrett (2001), I suggest that the discernible traits of the ethical planner are as follows:

1. The ethical planning practitioner is a respectable professional who:

- knows what the laws require and obeys them
- does not commit unethical acts
- seeks to avoid doing bad things
- is guided by integrity and a sense of what is right
- embraces obligations to others
- acts with due regard for individual and societal freedoms
- extends obligations beyond legal compliance
- assumes an attitude of stewardship and responsibility for protection and enhancement of human and natural resources

2. The ethical planning practitioner is a scholar of the AICP Code who:

- reads and rereads the AICP Code frequently, or at least every time an ethics question manifests
- monitors the professional institute for changes to, and interpretations of, the AICP Code, including any enforcement actions
- knows the AICP Code in the same way a zoning administrator knows a locality's zoning code
- applies the AICP Code with strict construction but also expands the narrow contexts of the rules of conduct to the broadest reasonable contexts
- respects the aspirational principles and never discards them as unenforceable
- attends continuing education sessions about ethics, and absorbs and applies the information gleaned
- recognizes that conflicts exist among principles, among rules of conduct, and between the principles and rules of conduct of the AICP Code
- is willing to seek advice from AICP's Ethics Officer

3. The ethical planning practitioner is a conscientious deliberator and prudent decision maker who:

- corrects his or her perspective, or that of another person, when thought processes are leading to the rationalization of a choice that the planner or the other person wants to make
- chooses the best approach when none of the available approaches will provide the ideal result
- resolves personal value conflicts ethically and legally, without sacrificing integrity
- adjusts his or her behavior in response to new information
- recognizes errors in judgment, including ethical mishaps
- recognizes that inaction, including omission, is a choice with ethical implications
- develops the capacity to meet ethical crises and prevent them before they arise

4. The ethical planning practitioner is an inspirational, professional role model who:

- sets the standard for normal conduct of planning and agency business
- is the epitome of integrity
- says "no" to all requests to do something unethical or illegal
- does not excuse others for unethical or illegal acts
- sees to it that those failing to serve the public office are removed from public service if they don't change their ways
- engages in preventive avoidance, such as keeping social distance from influential people, to reduce pressure for favoritism
- maintains and fosters open and honest communication
- devotes time generously to groups that need assistance, especially disadvantaged persons
- commits to serving the public interest and acts in accordance with the public interest
- exercises administrative discretion responsibly and consistently
- provides ways to ensure accountability of action and responsibility for actions
- finds ways to advance the public's positive association with the work of planners, not just to preserve the status quo of the profession in the public eye
- finds ways to positively reward others for their ethical behavior

APPENDICES

Appendix A: AICP Code of Ethics and Professional Conduct

Adopted March 19, 2005
Effective June 1, 2005
Revised October 3, 2009

We, professional planners, who are members of the American Institute of Certified Planners, subscribe to our Institute's Code of Ethics and Professional Conduct. Our Code is divided into four sections:

Section A contains a statement of aspirational principles that constitute the ideals to which we are committed. We shall strive to act in accordance with our stated principles. However, an allegation that we failed to achieve our aspirational principles cannot be the subject of a misconduct charge or be a cause for disciplinary action.

Section B contains rules of conduct to which we are held accountable. If we violate any of these rules, we can be the object of a charge of misconduct and shall have the responsibility of responding to and cooperating with the investigation and enforcement procedures. If we are found to be blameworthy by the AICP Ethics Committee, we shall be subject to the imposition of sanctions that may include loss of our certification.

Section C contains the procedural provisions of the Code. It (1) describes the way that one may obtain either a formal or informal advisory ruling, and (2) details how a charge of misconduct can be filed, and how charges are investigated, prosecuted, and adjudicated.

Section D contains procedural provisions that govern situations in which a planner is convicted of a serious crime.

The principles to which we subscribe in Sections A and B of the Code derive from the special responsibility of our profession to serve the public interest with compassion for the welfare of all people and, as professionals, to our obligation to act with high integrity.

As the basic values of society can come into competition with each other, so can the aspirational principles we espouse under this Code. An ethical judgment often requires a conscientious balancing, based on the facts and context of a particular situation and on the precepts of the entire Code.

As Certified Planners, all of us are also members of the American Planning Association and share in the goal of building better, more inclusive communities. We want the public to be aware of the principles by which we practice our profession in the quest of that goal. We sincerely hope that the public will respect the commitments we make to our employers and clients, our fellow professionals, and all other persons whose interests we affect.

A: Principles to Which We Aspire

1. Our Overall Responsibility to the Public

Our primary obligation is to serve the public interest and we, therefore, owe our allegiance to a conscientiously attained concept of the public interest that is formulated through continuous and open debate. We shall achieve high standards of professional integrity, proficiency, and knowledge. To comply with our obligation to the public, we aspire to the following principles:

a) We shall always be conscious of the rights of others.

b) We shall have special concern for the long-range consequences of present actions.

c) We shall pay special attention to the interrelatedness of decisions.

d) We shall provide timely, adequate, clear, and accurate information on planning issues to all affected persons and to governmental decision makers.

e) We shall give people the opportunity to have a meaningful impact on the development of plans and programs that may affect them. Participation should be broad enough to include those who lack formal organization or influence.

f) We shall seek social justice by working to expand choice and opportunity for all persons, recognizing a special responsibility to plan for the needs of the disadvantaged and to promote racial and economic integration. We shall urge the alteration of policies, institutions, and decisions that oppose such needs.

g) We shall promote excellence of design and endeavor to conserve and preserve the integrity and heritage of the natural and built environment.

h) We shall deal fairly with all participants in the planning process. Those of us who are public officials or employees shall also deal evenhandedly with all planning process participants.

2. Our Responsibility to Our Clients and Employers

We owe diligent, creative, and competent performance of the work we do in pursuit of our client or employer's interest. Such performance, however, shall always be consistent with our faithful service to the public interest.

a) We shall exercise independent professional judgment on behalf of our clients and employers.

b) We shall accept the decisions of our client or employer concerning the objectives and nature of the professional services we perform unless the course of action is illegal or plainly inconsistent with our primary obligation to the public interest.

c) We shall avoid a conflict of interest or even the appearance of a conflict of interest in accepting assignments from clients or employers.

3. Our Responsibility to Our Profession and Colleagues

We shall contribute to the development of, and respect for, our profession by improving knowledge and techniques, making work relevant to solutions of community problems, and increasing public understanding of planning activities.

a) We shall protect and enhance the integrity of our profession.

b) We shall educate the public about planning issues and their relevance to our everyday lives.

c) We shall describe and comment on the work and views of other professionals in a fair and professional manner.

d) We shall share the results of experience and research that contribute to the body of planning knowledge.

e) We shall examine the applicability of planning theories, methods, research and practice and standards to the facts and analysis of each particular situation and shall not accept the applicability of a customary solution without first establishing its appropriateness to the situation.

f) We shall contribute time and resources to the professional development of students, interns, beginning professionals, and other colleagues.

g) We shall increase the opportunities for members of underrepresented groups to become professional planners and help them advance in the profession.

h) We shall continue to enhance our professional education and training.

i) We shall systematically and critically analyze ethical issues in the practice of planning.

j) We shall contribute time and effort to groups lacking in adequate planning resources and to voluntary professional activities.

B: Our Rules of Conduct

We adhere to the following Rules of Conduct, and we understand that our Institute will enforce compliance with them. If we fail to adhere to these Rules, we could receive sanctions, the ultimate being the loss of our certification:

1. We shall not deliberately or with reckless indifference fail to provide adequate, timely, clear and accurate information on planning issues.

2. We shall not accept an assignment from a client or employer when the services to be performed involve conduct that we know to be illegal or in violation of these rules.

3. We shall not accept an assignment from a client or employer to publicly advocate a position on a planning issue that is indistinguishably adverse to a position we publicly advocated for a previous client or employer within the past three years unless (1) we determine in good faith after consultation with other qualified professionals that our change of position will not cause present detriment to our previous client or employer, and (2) we make full written disclosure of the conflict to our current client or employer and receive written permission to proceed with the assignment.

4. We shall not, as salaried employees, undertake other employment in planning or a related profession, whether or not for pay, without having made full written disclosure to the employer who furnishes our salary and having received subsequent written permission to undertake additional employment, unless our employer has a written policy which expressly dispenses with a need to obtain such consent.

5. We shall not, as public officials or employees, accept from anyone other than our public employer any compensation, commission, rebate, or other advantage that may be perceived as related to our public office or employment.

6. We shall not perform work on a project for a client or employer if, in addition to the agreed upon compensation from our client or employer, there is a possibility for direct personal or financial gain to us, our family members, or persons living in our household, unless our client or employer, after full written disclosure from us, consents in writing to the arrangement.

7. We shall not use to our personal advantage, nor that of a subsequent client or employer, information gained in a professional relationship that the client or employer has requested be held inviolate or that we should recognize as confidential because its disclosure could result in embarrassment or other detriment to the client or employer. Nor shall we disclose such confidential information except when (1) required by process of law, or (2) required to prevent a clear violation of law, or (3) required to prevent a substantial injury to the public. Disclosure pursuant to (2) and (3) shall not be made until after we have verified the facts and issues involved and, when practicable, exhausted efforts to obtain reconsideration of the matter and have sought separate opinions on the issue from other qualified professionals employed by our client or employer.

8. We shall not, as public officials or employees, engage in private communications with planning process participants if the discussions relate to a matter over which we have authority to make a binding, final determination if such private communications are prohibited by law or by agency rules, procedures, or custom.

9. We shall not engage in private discussions with decision makers in the planning process in any manner prohibited by law or by agency rules, procedures, or custom.

10. We shall neither deliberately, nor with reckless indifference, misrepresent the qualifications, views and findings of other professionals.

11. We shall not solicit prospective clients or employment through use of false or misleading claims, harassment, or duress.

12. We shall not misstate our education, experience, training, or any other facts which are relevant to our professional qualifications.

13. We shall not sell, or offer to sell, services by stating or implying an ability to influence decisions by improper means.

14. We shall not use the power of any office to seek or obtain a special advantage that is not a matter of public knowledge or is not in the public interest.

15. We shall not accept work beyond our professional competence unless the client or employer understands and agrees that such work will be performed by another professional competent to perform the work and acceptable to the client or employer.

16. We shall not accept work for a fee, or pro bono, that we know cannot be performed with the promptness required by the prospective client, or that is required by the circumstances of the assignment.

17. We shall not use the product of others' efforts to seek professional recognition or acclaim intended for producers of original work.

18. We shall not direct or coerce other professionals to make analyses or reach findings not supported by available evidence.

19. We shall not fail to disclose the interests of our client or employer when participating in the planning process. Nor shall we participate in an effort to conceal the true interests of our client or employer.

20. We shall not unlawfully discriminate against another person.

21. We shall not withhold cooperation or information from the AICP Ethics Officer or the AICP Ethics Committee if a charge of ethical misconduct has been filed against us.

22. We shall not retaliate or threaten retaliation against a person who has filed a charge of ethical misconduct against us or another planner, or who is cooperating in the Ethics Officer's investigation of an ethics charge.

23. We shall not use the threat of filing an ethics charge in order to gain, or attempt to gain, an advantage in dealings with another planner.

24. We shall not file a frivolous charge of ethical misconduct against another planner.

25. We shall neither deliberately, nor with reckless indifference, commit any wrongful act, whether or not specified in the Rules of Conduct, that reflects adversely on our professional fitness.

26. We shall not fail to immediately notify the Ethics Officer by both receipted Certified and Regular First Class Mail if we are convicted of a "serious crime" as defined in Section D of the Code; nor immediately following such conviction shall we represent ourselves as Certified Planners or Members of AICP until our membership is reinstated by the AICP Ethics Committee pursuant to the procedures in Section D of the Code.

C: Our Code Procedures

1. Introduction

In brief, our Code Procedures (1) describe the way that one may obtain either a formal or informal advisory ethics ruling, and (2) detail how a charge of misconduct can be filed, and how charges are investigated, prosecuted, and adjudicated.

2. Informal Advice

All of us are encouraged to seek informal ethics advice from the Ethics Officer. Informal advice is not given in writing and is not binding on AICP, but the AICP Ethics Committee shall take it into consideration in the event a charge of misconduct is later filed against us concerning the conduct in question. If we ask the Ethics Officer for informal advice and do not receive a response within 21 calendar days of our request, we should notify the Chair of the Ethics Committee that we are awaiting a response.

3. Formal Advice

Only the Ethics Officer is authorized to give formal advice on the propriety of a planner's proposed conduct. Formal advice is binding on AICP and any of us who can demonstrate that we followed such advice shall have a defense to any charge of misconduct. The advice will be issued to us in writing signed by the Ethics Officer. The written advice shall not include names or places without the written consent of all persons to be named. Requests for formal advice must be in writing and must contain sufficient details, real or hypothetical, to permit a definitive opinion. The Ethics Officer has the discretion to issue or not issue formal advice. The Ethics Officer will not issue formal advice if he or she determines that the request deals with past conduct that should be the subject of a charge of misconduct. The Ethics Officer will respond to requests for formal advice within 21 days of receipt and will docket the requests in a log that will be distributed on a quarterly basis to the Chair of the AICP Ethics Committee. If the Ethics Officer fails to furnish us with a timely response we should notify the Chair of the AICP Ethics Committee that we are awaiting a response.

4. Published Formal Advisory Rulings

The Ethics Officer shall transmit a copy of all formal advice to the AICP Ethics Committee. The Committee, from time to time, will determine if the formal advice provides guidance to the interpretation of the Code and should be published as a formal advisory ruling. Also, the Ethics Committee has the authority to draft and publish formal advisory rulings when it determines that guidance to interpretation of the Code is needed or desirable.

5. Filing a Charge of Misconduct

Any person, whether or not an AICP member, may file a charge of misconduct against a Certified Planner. A charge of misconduct shall be made in a letter sent to the AICP Ethics Officer. The letter may be signed or it may be anonymous. The person filing the charge is urged to maintain confidentiality to the extent practicable. The person filing the charge should not send a copy of the charge to the Certified Planner identified in the letter or to any other person. The letter shall accurately identify the Certified Planner against whom the charge is being made and describe the conduct that allegedly violated the provisions of the Rules of Conduct. The person filing a charge should also cite all provisions of the Rules of Conduct that have allegedly been violated. However, a charge will not be dismissed if the Ethics Officer is able to determine from the facts stated in the letter that certain Rules of Conduct may have been violated. The letter reciting the charge should be accompanied by all relevant documentation available to the person filing the charge. While anonymously filed charges are permitted, anonymous filers will not receive notification of the disposition of the charge. Anonymous filers may furnish a postal address in the event the Ethics Officer needs to reach them for an inquiry.

6. Receipt of Charge by Ethics Officer

The Ethics Officer shall maintain a log of all letters containing charges of misconduct filed against Certified Planners upon their receipt and shall transmit a quarterly report of such correspondence to the Chair of the Ethics Committee. Within two weeks of receipt of a charge, the Ethics Officer shall prepare a cover letter and transmit the charge and all attached documentation to the named Certified Planner, who shall be now referred to as "the Respondent." The Ethics Officer's cover letter shall indicate whether the Ethics Officer expects the Respondent to file a "preliminary response" or whether the Ethics Officer is summarily dismissing the charge because it is clearly without merit. A copy of the cover letter will also be sent to the Charging Party, if identified. If the cover letter summarily dismisses the charge, it shall be sent to an identifiable Charging Party by receipted Certified Mail. The Charging Party will have the right to appeal the summary dismissal as provided in Section 11. After the Ethics Officer has received a charge, the Charging Party may withdraw it only with the permission of the Ethics Officer. After receiving a charge, the Ethics Officer shall have a duty to keep an identified Charging Party informed of its status. If an identified Charging Party has not received a status report from the Ethics Officer for 60 calendar days, the Charging Party should notify the Chair of the AICP Ethics Committee of the lapse.

7. Right of Counsel

A planner who receives a charge of misconduct under a cover letter requesting a preliminary response should understand that if he or she desires legal representation, it would be advisable to obtain such representation at the earliest point in the procedure. However, a planner who elects to proceed at first without legal representation will not be precluded from engaging such representation at any later point in the procedure.

8. Preliminary Responses to a Charge of Misconduct

If the Ethics Officer requests a preliminary response, the Respondent shall be allowed 30 calendar days from receipt of the Ethics Officer's letter to send the response to the Ethics Officer. The Ethics Officer will grant an extension of time, not to exceed 15 calendar days, if the request for the extension is made within the 30 day period. Failure to make a timely preliminary response constitutes a failure to cooperate with the Ethics Officer's investigation of the charge. A preliminary response should include documentation, the names, addresses and telephone numbers of witnesses, and all of the facts and arguments that counter the charge. Because the motivation of the person who filed the charge is irrelevant, the Respondent should not discuss it. The Ethics Officer will send a copy of the preliminary response to the Charging Party, if identified, and allow the Charging Party 15 calendar days from the date of receipt to respond.

9. Conducting an Investigation

After review of the preliminary response from the Respondent and any counter to that response furnished by an identified Charging Party, or if no timely preliminary response is received, the Ethics Officer shall decide whether an investigation is appropriate. If the Ethics Officer determines that an investigation should be conducted, he or she may designate a member of the AICP staff or AICP counsel to conduct the investigation. The Respondent must cooperate in the investigation and encourage others with relevant information, whether favorable or unfavorable, to cooperate. Neither the Ethics Officer, nor designee, will make credibility findings to resolve differing witness versions of facts in dispute.

10. Dismissal of Charge or Issuance of Complaint

If, with or without an investigation, the charge appears to be without merit, the Ethics Officer shall dismiss it in a letter, giving a full explanation of the reasons. The dismissal letter shall be sent to the Respondent and the Charging Party by receipted Certified Mail. If, however, the Ethics Officer's investigation indicates that a Complaint is warranted, the Ethics Officer shall draft a Complaint and send it to the Respondent by receipted Certified Mail, with a copy to the Charging Party. The Complaint shall consist of numbered paragraphs containing recitations of alleged facts. Following the fact paragraphs, there shall be numbered paragraphs of alleged violations, which shall cite provisions of the Rules of Conduct that the Ethics Officer believes are implicated. The allegations in the Complaint shall be based on the results of the Ethics Officer's investigation of the charge and may be additional to, or different from, those allegations initially relied upon by the Charging Party. The Ethics Officer shall maintain a log of all dismissals and shall transmit the log on a quarterly basis to the Chair of the Ethics Committee.

11. Appeal of Dismissal of Charge

Identified Charging Parties who are notified of the dismissal of their ethics charges shall have 30 calendar days from the date of the receipt of their dismissal letters to file an appeal with the Ethics Committee. The appeal shall be sent to the Ethics Officer who shall record it in a log and transmit it within 21 calendar days to the Ethics Committee. The Ethics Committee shall either affirm or reverse the dismissal. If the dismissal is reversed, the Ethics Committee shall either direct the Ethics Officer to conduct a further investigation and review the charge again, or issue a Complaint based on the materials before the Committee. The Ethics Officer shall notify the Charging Party and the Respondent of the Ethics Committee's determination.

12. Answering a Complaint

The Respondent shall have 30 calendar days from receipt of a Complaint in which to file an Answer. An extension not to exceed 15 calendar days will be granted if the request is made within the 30 day period. In furnishing an Answer, the Respondent is expected to cooperate in good faith. General denials are un-acceptable. The Answer must specifically admit or deny each of the fact allegations in the Complaint. It is acceptable to deny a fact allegation on the ground that the planner is unable to verify its correctness, but that explanation should be stated as the reason for denial. The failure of a Respondent to make a timely denial of any fact alleged in the Complaint shall be deemed an admission of such fact. The Ethics Officer may amend a Complaint to delete any disputed fact, whether or not material to the issues. The Ethics Officer also may amend a Complaint to restate fact allegations by verifying and adopting the Respondent's version of what occurred. The Ethics Officer shall send the Complaint or Amended Complaint and the Respondent's Answer to the Ethics Committee with a copy to an identified Charging Party. The Ethics Officer shall also inform the Ethics Committee if there are any disputed material facts based on a comparison of the documents.

13. Conducting a Hearing

a) If the Ethics Officer notifies the Ethics Committee that material facts are in dispute or if the Ethics Committee, on its own, finds that to be the case, the Chair of the Committee shall designate a "Hearing Official" from among the membership of the Committee. At this point in the process, the Ethics Officer, either personally or through a designated AICP staff member or AICP counsel, shall continue to serve as both Investigator-Prosecutor and as the Clerk serving the Ethics Committee, the Hearing Official and the Respondent. In carrying out clerical functions, the Ethics Officer, or designee, may discuss with the Ethics Committee and the Hearing Official the procedural arrange-ments for the hearing. Until the Ethics Committee decides the case, however, the Ethics Officer or designee shall not discuss the merits of the case with any member of the Committee unless the Respondent is present or is afforded an equal opportunity to address the Committee member.

b) The Ethics Officer shall transmit a "Notice of Hearing" to the Respondent, the Hearing Official and an identified Charging Party. The hearing shall normally be conducted in the vicinity where the alleged misconduct occurred. The Notice will contain a list of all disputed material facts that need to be resolved. The hearing will be confined to resolution of those facts. There shall be no requirement that formal rules of evidence be observed.

c) The Ethics Officer will have the burden of proving, by a preponderance of the evidence, that misconduct occurred. The Ethics Officer may present witness testimony and any other evidence relevant to demonstrating the existence of each disputed material fact. The Respondent will then be given the opportunity to present witness testimony and any other evidence relevant to controvert the testimony and other evidence submitted by the Ethics Officer. The Ethics Officer may then be given an opportunity to present additional witness testimony and other evidence in rebuttal. All witnesses who testify for the Ethics Officer or the Respondent shall be subject to cross-examination by the other party. The Hearing Official shall make an electronic recording of the hearing and shall make copies of the recording available to the Ethics Officer and the Respondent.

d) At least 30 calendar days before the hearing, the Ethics Officer and the Respondent shall exchange lists of proposed witnesses who will testify, and copies of all exhibits that will be introduced, at the hearing. There shall be no other discovery and no pre-hearing motions. All witnesses must testify in person at the hearing unless arrangements can be made by agreement between the Respondent and the Ethics Officer prior to the hearing, or by ruling of the Hearing Official during the hearing, to have an unavailable witness's testimony submitted in a video recording that permits the Hearing Official to observe the demeanor of the witness. No unavailable witness's testimony shall be admissible unless the opposing party was offered a meaningful opportunity to cross-examine the witness. The hearing shall not be open to the public. The Hearing Official shall have the discretion to hold open the hearing to accept recorded video testimony of unavailable witnesses. The Respondent will be responsible for the expense of bringing his or her witnesses to the hearing or to have their testimony video recorded. Following the closing of the hearing, the Hearing Official shall make findings only as to the disputed material facts and transmit the findings to the full Ethics Committee, the Ethics Officer, and the Respondent. The Hearing Official, prior to issuing findings, may request that the parties submit proposed findings of fact for his or her consideration.

14. Deciding the Case

The Ethics Committee (including the Hearing Official member of the Committee) shall resolve the ethics matter by reviewing the documentation that sets out the facts that were not in dispute, any fact findings that were required to be made by a Hearing Official, and any arguments submitted to it by the Respondent and the Ethics Officer. The Ethics Officer shall give 45 calendar days notice to the Respondent of the date of the Ethics Committee meeting during which the matter will be resolved. The Ethics Officer and the Respondent shall have 21 calendar days to submit memoranda stating their positions. The Ethics Officer shall transmit the memoranda to the Ethics Committee no later than 15 calendar days prior to the scheduled meeting. If the Committee determines that the Rules of Conduct have not been violated, it shall dismiss the Complaint and direct the Ethics Officer to notify the Respondent and an identified Charging Party. If the Ethics Committee determines that the Ethics Officer has demonstrated that the Rules of Conduct have been violated, it shall also determine the appropriate sanction, which shall either be a reprimand, suspension, or expulsion. The Ethics Committee shall direct the Ethics Officer to notify the Respondent and an identified Charging Party of its action and to draft a formal explanation of its decision and the discipline chosen. Upon approval of the Ethics Committee, the explanation and discipline chosen shall be published and titled "Opinion of the AICP Ethics Committee." The determination of the AICP Ethics Committee shall be final.

15. Settlement of Charges

a) Prior to issuance of a Complaint, the Ethics Officer may negotiate a settlement between the Respondent and an identified Charging Party if the Ethics Officer determines that the Charging Party has been personally aggrieved by the alleged misconduct of the Respondent and a private resolution between the two would not be viewed as compromising Code principles. If a settlement is reached under such circumstances, the Charging Party will be allowed to withdraw the charge of misconduct.

b) Also prior to issuance of a Complaint, the Ethics Officer may enter into a proposed settlement agreement without the participation of an identified Charging Party. However, in such circumstances, the proposed settlement agreement shall be contingent upon the approval of the Ethics Committee. An identified Charging Party will be given notice and an opportunity to be heard by the Ethics Committee before it votes to approve or disapprove the proposed pre-Complaint settlement.

c) After issuance of a Complaint by the Ethics Officer, a settlement can be negotiated solely between the Ethics Officer and the Respondent, subject to the approval of the Ethics Committee without input from an identified Charging Party.

16. Resignations and Lapses of Membership

If an AICP member who is the subject of a Charge of Misconduct resigns or allows membership to lapse prior to a final determination of the Charge (and any Complaint that may have issued), the ethics matter will be held in abeyance subject to being revived if the individual applies for reinstatement of membership within two years. If such former member, however, fails to apply for reinstatement within two years, the individual shall not be permitted to reapply for certification for a period of 10 years from the date of resignation or lapse of membership. If the Ethics Officer receives a Charge of Misconduct against a former member, the Ethics Officer shall make an effort to locate and advise the former member of the filing of the Charge and this Rule of Procedure.

17. Annual Report of Ethics Officer

Prior to January 31 of each calendar year the Ethics Officer shall publish an Annual Report of all ethics activity during the preceding calendar year to the AICP Ethics Committee and the AICP Commission. The AICP Commission shall make the Annual Report available to the membership.

D: Planners Convicted of Serious Crimes—Automatic Suspension of Certification

1. Automatic Suspension Upon Conviction for "Serious Crime"

We acknowledge that if we are convicted of a "serious crime," our certification and membership shall be automatically suspended indefinitely. The automatic suspension applies whether the conviction resulted from a plea of guilty or nolo contendere or from a verdict after trial or otherwise, and regardless of the pendency of any appeal. A "serious crime" shall include any crime a necessary element of which, as determined by the statutory or common law definition of such crime in the jurisdiction where the judgment was entered, involves false swearing, misrepresentation, fraud, willful failure to file income tax returns or to pay the tax, deceit, bribery, extortion, misappropriation, theft, conflict of interest, or an attempt to or a conspiracy or solicitation of another to commit a "serious crime."

2. Duty to Notify Ethics Officer When Convicted of "Serious Crime."

As required by Rule of Conduct 26, in Section B of the Code, we shall notify the Ethics Officer both by receipted Certified and Regular First Class Mail if we are convicted of a "serious crime" as defined in Paragraph 1. We understand that failure to do so shall result in a delay in the commencement of the one year waiting period for filing reinstatement petitions as provided for in Paragraph 3.

3. Petition for Reinstatement of Certification and Membership

Upon learning of the conviction of a Certified Planner for a serious crime, the Ethics Officer shall send the convicted individual by receipted Certified and Regular First Class Mail to the last address of record a Notice Of Suspension of AICP Membership and Certification. The Notice shall advise the individual that one year from the date of the Notice, but in no event prior to release from incarceration, he or she may petition the AICP Ethics Committee for reinstatement. A Petition for Reinstatement shall be sent to the Ethics Officer, who shall forward it to the Ethics Committee. The Ethics Committee shall in its sole judgment determine whether reinstatement is appropriate and if so whether and what conditions shall be applied to such reinstatement. The Ethics Officer shall transmit the reinstatement determination to the petitioner. If the Ethics Committee denies the Petition, the Ethics Officer shall transmit the denial to the petitioner along with notice that the petitioner shall have the opportunity to file a subsequent petition after 12 months from the date of the Ethics Committee's determination.

4. Publication of Conviction for Serious Crime:

If, while we are Certified Planners, we are convicted of a serious offense, as defined in Paragraph 1, we authorize the Ethics Officer to publish our name and a description of the crime we committed in a publication of AICP and of the American Planning Association. This authority to publish shall survive the voluntary or involuntary termination or suspension of our AICP membership and certification.

Appendix B: State Ethics Laws Applicable to Local Government Employees

Practicing planners are expected to be aware of and heed ethics laws in their states. Many states have established ethics commissions and have passed ethics laws. However, in general, states limit the application of their ethics laws to legislators and state employees. Planners working for states are most likely already aware of these laws, so this appendix identifies only those states with ethics standards that extend to local government employees and specifically planners. The National Conference of State Legislatures (ncsl.org) has thoroughly researched the state laws on legislative ethics and lobbying, and provides links to the statutes.

Readers should not rely on the summaries below for official applications but should view them as representative of the types of ethical issues that are addressed by state laws as applied to employees at the local government level. States are listed in alphabetical order. Each entry includes the title and citation of the legislation, along with a summary of salient ethics provisions.

Alabama

Alabama Code, Title 36, Chapter 25, "Code of Ethics for Public Officials, Employees, Etc.," defines "public employee" as "any person employed at the state, county, or municipal level of government or their instrumentalities" (§36-25-1). Prohibitions are specified, including against the use of official position or office by a public employee for personal gain, and the use of equipment, facilities, time, materials, human labor, or other public property for private benefit or business benefit (§36-25-5).

Arizona

Arizona Revised Statutes, Title 38, "Public Officers and Employees," defines "office," "board," or "commission" as "any office, board or commission of the state, or any political subdivision thereof" (§38-101). It addresses conflicts of interest and specifically pertains to "all public officers and employees of incorporated cities or towns, of political subdivisions and of the state and any of its departments, commissions, agencies, bodies or boards" (§38-501). Public officials must make known any interests in contracts or in decisions to be made by the agency (§38-503). Prohibited acts include disclosure of certain information, use of office to secure any valuable thing or valuable benefit, and representation of interests before public agencies by which the officer is, or was, employed within the past 12 months (§38-504).

Arkansas

Arkansas Code of 1987 Annotated, Title 21, "Public Officers and Employees," Chapter 8, "Ethics and Conflicts of Interest," defines "governmental body" to include not only the state but any municipality, county, school district, improvement district, or any political district or subdivision thereof (§21-8-301). In addition to being subject to certain disclosure prohibitions, a public servant is prohibited from using, or attempting to use, his or her "official position to secure special privileges or exemptions for himself or herself or his or her spouse, child, parents, or other persons standing in the first degree of relationship, or for those with whom he or she has a substantial financial relationship that is not available to others except as may be otherwise provided by law" (§21-8-304).

California

California Government Code, Title 9, Chapter 7, "Conflict of Interest," and Chapter 9.5, "Ethics," provide salient provisions. Government Code §87100 provides that "no public official at any level of state or local government shall make, participate in making or in any way attempt to use his official position to influence a governmental decision in which he knows or has reason to know he has a financial interest." Honorariums are also limited—"No elected state officer, elected officer of a local government agency, or other individual specified in Section 87200" shall accept any honorarium (§89502)—as are gifts "from any single source in any calendar year with a total value of more than $250" (§89503). There are also specific limits on the use of travel funds (§89506). Section 87200 applies to, among others, members of planning commissions, chief administrative officers of counties, mayors, city managers, city attorneys, city treasurers, chief administrative officers and members of city councils, and other public officials who manage public investments.

Florida

Florida Statutes, Title X, "Public Officers, Employees and Records," Chapter 112, "Public Officials and Employees: General Provisions," Part III, "Code of Ethics for Public Officers and Employees," contains salient provisions, such as, "No officer or employee of a state agency or of a county, city, or other political subdivision of the state, and no member of the Legislature or legislative employee, shall have any interest, financial or otherwise, direct or indirect; engage in any business transaction or professional activity; or incur any obligation of any nature which is in substantial conflict with the proper discharge of his or her duties in the public interest (§112-311(5)). Section 112-313 specifies standards of conduct for "public officers," defined as "any person[s] elected or appointed to hold office in any agency, including any person serving on an advisory body." Limitations include solicitation of gifts, doing business with one's agency, misuse of public employment, conflicting employment or contractual relationships, and disclosure of information.

Georgia

Georgia Code, Title 45, "Public Officers and Employees," Chapter 10, "Codes of Ethics and Conflicts of Interest," Article 1, "Code of Ethics," Section 45-10-1, "Code of Ethics for Government Service," establishes a code of ethics for government service applicable to all governments in the state. The code is very brief, with just 10 principles.

Idaho

Idaho Code Title 59, "Public Officers in General," Chapter 7, "Ethics in Government Act of 1990," contains provisions that apply to any public official at any level of government (§59-702). The law includes a conflict-of-interest provision: "A public official shall not take any official action or make a formal decision or formal recommendation concerning any matter where he has a conflict of interest and has failed to disclose such conflict" (§59-704).

Iowa

Iowa Code, Title II, Subtitle 2, Chapter 68B, "Conflicts of Interest of Public Officers and Employees," "Iowa Public Officials Act" (§68B.1), addresses ethics. A conflict-of-interest provision applies to "any person who serves or is employed by the state or a political subdivision of the state" and provides that persons "shall not engage in any outside employment or activity which is in conflict with the person's official duties and responsibilities" (§68B.2A).

Louisiana

Louisiana Revised Statutes, Title 42, "Public Officers and Employees," defines "public office" as "any state, district, parish or municipal office, elective or appointive, or any position as member on a board or commission, elective or appointive, when the office or position is established by the constitution or laws of this state" (§42.1). Chapter 15, "Code of Governmental Ethics," applies to officials and employees of the state and its political subdivisions (§42.110). The code includes limitations on payment from nonpublic sources (§42.1111); participation in transactions in which one has a personal substantial economic interest (§42.1112); gifts (§42.1115); receipt of food, drink, and refreshments (§42.1115.1); abuse of office (§42.1116); and illegal payments of anything of economic value (§42.1117).

Massachusetts

Massachusetts General Laws, Chapter 268A, "Conduct of Public Officials and Employees," has ethics provisions. State, county, and municipal employees are subject to this law, which describes corrupt gifts (§2), gifts or promises of value (§3), and other ethics topics.

Michigan

Michigan Compiled Laws, Chapter 15, "Public Officers and Employees," includes standards of conduct for public officers and employees (§15.341–48). Although the law applies only to state employees, there is a whistle-blower provision (§15.342.b) that extends protection to employees of the state and its political subdivisions (§15.341, definition of "employee").

Mississippi

Mississippi Code, Title 25, "Public Officers and Employees," Chapter 4, "Ethics in Government," Article 3, "Conflicts of Interest; Improper Use of Office," defines "government" to include counties and municipalities (§25-4-103). Certain actions, activities, and business relationships are prohibited (§25-4-105).

Missouri

Missouri Revised Statutes, Chapter 105, "Public Officers and Employees—Miscellaneous Provisions," applies to employees of any political subdivision of the state per the definition of "political subdivision" (§105.450). Certain acts are prohibited (§105.452, §105.454).

Montana

Montana Code Annotated, Title 2, "Government Structure and Administration," Chapter 2, "Standards of Conduct," contains a Code of Ethics (Part 1) (§2-2-101) that defines "public employee" to include local government employees (§2-2-102). Section 2-2-104 establishes rules of conduct, which include limitations on disclosure of confidential information, acceptance of gifts of substantial value, and acceptance of salaries from more than one public position. Section 2-2-105 contains provisions limiting business relationships and certain advantageous employment with public agencies.

Nevada

Nevada Revised Statutes, Title 23, "Public Officers and Employees," Chapter 281A, "Ethics in Government," Nevada Ethics in Government Law, Section 281A.010, contains salient provisions. "Political subdivision" means any county, city, or other local government (§281A.145); and "public employee" is defined to include county and city employees (§281A.150). A code of ethics is established (§281A.400); limitations include acceptance of certain gifts, participation in contracts when there is a pecuniary interest, and the use of public information.

New Mexico

New Mexico Laws, Chapter 10, "Public Officers and Employees," Article 16, "Governmental Conduct," Governmental Conduct Act (§10-16-1), defines "public officer or employee" to include employees of local government agencies (§10-16-2). Ethical principles are established (§10-16-3) and certain activities are regulated, including official actions for private gain and acceptance of certain gifts (§10-16-4), honorariums for public duties (§10-16-4.1), certain employment activities (§10-16-4.3), and disclosure of confidential information (§10-16-6).

Ohio

Ohio Revised Code, Title 1, "State Government," Chapter 102, "Public Officers—Ethics," defines "public official or employee" to include any employee of any public agency (with some stated exceptions) and defines "public agency" to include counties, cities, villages, and townships (§102.01). Section 102.03 provides limitations on representation by present or former public officials or employees, use of authority to secure something of value, acceptance of gifts, and improper influences, among others.

Oregon

Oregon Revised Statutes, Chapter 244, "Government Ethics," Section 244.020, "Definitions," defines "public official" to include any person serving any of the state's political subdivisions. Ethics provisions include restrictions on gifts (§244.025), prohibitions on use of official positions (§244.040), and conflicts of interest (§244.120).

Pennsylvania

Pennsylvania Consolidated Statutes, Title 65, "Public Officers," Chapter 11, "Ethics Standards and Financial Disclosure," contains the "Public Official and Employee Ethics Act" (§65-1101). "Public officials" includes "most local officials" (§65-1101.1). The term "public employee[s]" is specifically defined to include individual employees of political subdivisions who are responsible for taking or recommending official action of a nonministerial nature with regard to planning and zoning, among other things (§65-1102). The law restricts activities, including those related to conflict of interest, improper influence, and honorariums (§65-1103).

Rhode Island

Rhode Island General Laws, Title 36, "Public Officers and Employees," Chapter 36-14, "Code of Ethics," defines "employees of state and local government," "municipal agency," and "state or municipal appointed official" (§36-14-2). Sections 36-14-4 to 36-14-7 constitute the Rhode Island Code of Ethics in Government (§36-14-3), to which state and municipal appointed officials and employees of state and local government, boards, commissions, and agencies are subject (§36-14-4). Prohibited activities are specified in §36-14-5 and include, but are not limited to, conflicts of interest, use of confidential information, and representation of others.

South Carolina

South Carolina Code, Title 8, "Public Officers and Employees," Chapter 13, "Ethics, Government Accountability, and Campaign Reform," defines "public employee" to include "a person employed by the State, a county, a municipality, or a political subdivision thereof" (§8-13-100). Rules of conduct are specified, including rules relating to conflicts of interest (§8-13-700), the giving or receiving of things of value (§8-13-705), the use or disclosure of confidential information (§8-13-725), representation before governmental entities (§8-13-740), and restrictions on employment in a field of former service (§8-13-755).

Tennessee

Tennessee Code Annotated, Title 8, "Public Officers and Employees," Chapter 17, "Ethical Standards for Officials and Employees," includes the legislative intent that "the integrity of the processes of local government be secured and protected from abuse" (§8-17-101). The statutes define officials and employees to include those of counties and municipalities (§8-17-102). Section 8-17-103, "Adoption of Ethical Standards," requires that "the governing body of each entity covered by this chapter shall adopt by ordinance or resolution, as appropriate, ethical standards for all officials and employees of such entity" (§8-17-103). Models of ethical standards for officials and employees are required to be prepared and disseminated to employees and officials (§8-17-105). Members of a governing body of an entity covered by the law who fail to adopt ethical standards are subject to removal from office (§8-17-106).

West Virginia

West Virginia Code, Chapter 6B, "Public Officers and Employees: Ethics; Conflicts of Interests; Disclosure" includes the "West Virginia Governmental Ethics Act" (§6B-1-1). It states the legislative intent to "maintain confidence in the integrity and impartiality of the governmental process in the state of West Virginia and its political subdivisions" (§6B-1-2). Further, it declares that "the decisions and actions of public officials and public employees must be made free from undue influence, favoritism or threat, at every level of government" (§6B-1-2). "Public employee" is defined as "any full-time or part-time employee of any state, county or municipal governmental body or any political subdivision thereof, including county school boards" (§6B-1-3). However, the act itself does not contain any specific standards of ethical conduct.

REFERENCES

American Institute of Certified Planners. 2009. Rev. ed. AICP Code of Ethics and Professional Conduct. Available at www.planning.org/ethics/ethicscode.htm.

American Planning Association. 1992. Ethical Principles in Planning. Adopted by the APA Board of Directors, May.

———. 2012. Ethics in Planning: A Toolkit for Conducting Ethics Sessions. Available at www.planning.org/ethics/pdf/apaethicstoolkit.pdf.

Barrett, Carol. 2002. *Everyday Ethics for Practicing Planners.* Chicago: APA Planners Press.

Bolan, Richard S. 1983. "The Structure of Ethical Choice in Planning Practice." *Journal of Planning Education and Research* 3: 23–34.

Carolin, Paulette M., Kimberly K. Gerhart-Fritz, and Jerry Weitz. 2012. "Ethical Challenges for Planning Consultants." Session at the APA National Planning Conference, Los Angeles. April 17.

Edison Research and Arbitron. June 2012. The Smartphone Consumer 2012.

Ethics Resource Center. 2008. *Ethics Resource Center's National Government Ethics Survey: An Inside View of Public Sector Ethics.* Arlington, Va.: Ethics Resource Center.

File, Thom, and Camille Ryan. 2014. "Computer and Internet Use in the United States: 2013." Current Population Survey Reports, P20-568. Washington, D.C.: U.S. Census Bureau.

Finkler, Earl. 1971. *Dissent and Independent Initiative in Planning Offices.* Planning Advisory Service Report no. 269. Chicago: American Society of Planning Officials.

Howe, Elizabeth. 1994. Acting on Ethics in City Planning. New Brunswick, N.J.: Center for Urban Policy Research, Rutgers University.

Howe, Elizabeth, and Jerome L. Kaufman. 1979. "The Ethics of Contemporary American Planners." *Journal of the American Planning Association* 45(3): 243–55.

Marcuse, Peter. 1976. "Professional Ethics and Beyond: Values in Planning." *Journal of the American Institute of Planners* 42(3): 264–74.

Perego, Martha. 2008. "Ethics: Investing in Your Community." Public Management 90(10). Available at http://webapps.icma.org/pm/9010/public/ethics.cfm.

Salkin, Patricia E., and Julie A. Tappendorf. 2011. "Social Media and Ethics." American Planning Association Audio/Web Conference. Available at www.planning.org/store/product/?ProductCode =STR_TSME.

Steinberg, Sheldon S., and David T. Austern. 1990. *Government, Ethics, and Managers: A Guide to Solving Ethical Dilemmas in the Public Sector.* Westport, Conn.: Quorum Books.

Wachs, Martin, ed. 1985. *Ethics in Planning.* New Brunswick, N.J.: Center for Urban Policy Research, Rutgers University.

SCENARIO INDEXES

Index of AICP Code Principles to Which We Aspire in the Scenarios

Principles to Which We Aspire	Frequency in Scenarios	Scenarios in Which this Principle is Cited as Relevant
1.a. Consider rights of others	8	S18, S42, S43, S44, S47, S54
1.b. Concern for long-range consequences	4	S34, S35
1.c. Attend to interrelatedness of decisions	2	S34, S35
1.d. Provide information to all affected	17	S10, S21, S33, S35, S36, S38, S40, S46, S48, S55, S56, S59
1.e. Participation—meaningful impact	10	S5, S9, S26, S27, S29, S30, S38, S45, S53
1.f. Social justice—plan for disadvantaged	14	S5, S7, S8, S9, S13, S20, S26, S27, S28, S29, S33, S38, S53
1.g. Excellent design; preserve heritage	8	S4, S35, S36, S40, S53, S54
1.h. Deal fairly and evenhandedly	15	S2, S5, S24, S28, S33, S37, S40, S44, S46, S48, S53, S61, S64
2.a. Exercise independent judgment	22	S1, S2, S5, S6, S7, S8, S9, S10, S20, S21, S26, S27, S28, S36, S40, S41, S46, S52, S53, S64
2.b. Accept client decision unless illegal . . .	21	S2, S3, S5, S6, S7, S8, S9, S10, S26, S27, S28, S35, S36, S37, S44, S46, S48, S51
2.c. Avoid appearance of conflict of interest	18	S3, S13, S14, S15, S16, S17, S45, S46, S51, S52, S64, S69, S71, S73
3.a. Enhance professional integrity	12	S18, S46, S63, S64, S71
3.b. Educate public on planning issues	7	S1, S13, S26, S33, S35, S44, S61
3.c. Treat other professionals fairly	8	S1, S2, S8, S10, S43, S44, S48
3.d. Share experience and research	4	S35, S38, S54, S66
3.e. Apply customary solutions with caution	2	S4, S25
3.f. Contribute to professional development	5	S7, S12, S30, S32, S44
3.g. Increase opportunity for underrepresented groups	3	S7, S31, S32
3.h. Enhance education and training	1	S68
3.i. Examine/analyze ethical issues	0	
3.j. Contribute to those lacking resources	5	S9, S13, S26, S29

Index of AICP Code Rules of Conduct in the Scenarios

Rules of Conduct	Frequency in Scenarios	Scenarios in Which this Rule is Cited as Relevant
1. Inaccurate information—untruthfulness	15	S4, S6, S10, S29, S36, S37, S38, S39, S40, S41, S53, S54, S56, S57, S68
2. Illegal or unethical conduct	13	S2, S3, S4, S16, S23, S41, S45, S46, S47, S48, S61, S63
3. Change of public position on an issue	4	S4, S15, S16
4. Outside employment ("moonlighting")	12	S11, S12, S13, S14, S16, S45, S46, S49, S50, S51, S63, S73
5. Acceptance of gifts or advantage	11	S15, S51, S63, S64, S65, S66, S69, S70, S71, S72, S73
6. Personal or financial gain	4	S16, S52, S71, S73
7. Breach of confidentiality	7	S13, S16, S51, S53, S54, S55, S56
8. Private communication (public)	7	S15, S17, S47, S64, S69, S70
9. Private communication (other)	3	S6, S37, S69
10. Misrepresentation of others' qualifications	7	S8, S38, S41, S42, S48, S61, S74
11. Solicitation via false claims; duress	6	S12, S16, S19, S43, S47, S58, S63, S70
12. Misstatement of one's qualifications	6	S41, S43, S58, S60, S63, S68, S70
13. Influence via improper means	5	S15, S16, S41, S69, S70
14. Official power used for advantage	14	S11, S15, S45, S51, S52, S63, S64, S67, S68, S69, S71, S73, S74
15. Work beyond professional competence	2	S57, S58
16. Promptness of work required	4	S59, S60, S61, S63
17. Misuse of others' work	1	S43
18. Pressure: unsubstantiated findings	7	S8, S36, S41, S44, S46, S52, S57
19. Concealment of interest/ failure to disclose	12	S6, S8, S15, S16, S35, S41, S44, S51, S53, S61, S68
20. Unlawful discrimination	2	S18, S47
21. Cooperation in AICP investigation	1	S76
22. Retaliation for misconduct charge	2	S74, S75
23. Threat to file charge (advantage)	0	
24. No frivolous ethics charge	2	S8, S75
25. Deliberate, wrongful act	10	S12, S16, S41, S45, S46, S51, S52, S63, S67, S69
26. Notification of "serious crime"	0	

Selected Subjects Index

Community development: S5, S20, S37
Consulting: S4, S11, S15, S19, S22, S26, S27, S43, S45, S47, S50, S51, S57, S59, S60, S63, S66, S70
Environmental impact: S4, S36, S51, S57
Grant administration: S20, S23
Housing: S8, S9, S13, S25, S28
Transportation: S29, S38
Zoning administration: S2, S3, S12, S18, S24, S39, S40, S42, S46, S51, S52, S54, S55, S56, S58, S64

INDEX

For Product Safety Concerns and Information please contact our EU
representative GPSR@taylorandfrancis.com
Taylor & Francis Verlag GmbH, Kaufingerstraße 24, 80331 München, Germany

* 9 7 8 1 1 3 8 7 3 5 2 1 7 *